Why You Spend

The Invisible Triggers Controlling Your Money Habits

The moment you see your spending not as a math problem, but as a mirror of your mind, everything changes. Awareness is the first currency of wealth.

By: Ed Merid

Table of Contents

INTRODUCTION: The Science of Money You Never Learned

On a quiet Tuesday, Emily tapped her phone twice and spent $74 she hadn't planned to. A throw blanket she didn't need. A latte subscription she forgot she signed up for. By Friday, she couldn't tell you where half her paycheck went , only that her credit card balance had crept up again, and a dull anxiety sat in her chest.

She's not irresponsible. She's normal.

Here's the truth most financial advice ignores:
You don't spend money logically. You spend it emotionally. Automatically. Subconsciously.

In a world engineered for frictionless consumption ,where your environment, apps, and emotions collaborate to push you toward impulse , traditional budgeting doesn't stand a chance. Budgeting is like bringing a calculator to a poker game where the house controls your hormones.

Behind every swipe, tap, or "Buy Now" button is a hidden trigger:

- A push notification timed to your boredom
- A product placed at eye level to hijack your instincts
- A voice in your head whispering, *"You deserve this"*, right when your willpower is lowest

This book is not about guilt. It's not about spreadsheets, sacrifice, or shame.
It's about **power**.

When you understand what's *really* driving your financial decisions, the invisible forces, mental shortcuts, and emotional reflexes , you unlock something life-changing: *choice*. Not forced frugality, but conscious spending rooted in your values and your vision.

"Why You Spend" will show you how to decode your money habits, expose the psychological traps designed to drain you, and build mental resilience in a world of endless temptation.

Because once you see the triggers, **you can finally pull your own.**

Welcome to the part of money no one ever taught you , but that will change everything.

Let's begin.

PART 1: THE MIND UNDER THE MONEY

Imagine this: You're standing in line at a café. You're tired. You didn't sleep well. You scroll through your phone, notice a friend's vacation photo, and without really thinking, you tack on a pastry to your coffee order. Just a little treat. You deserve it, right?

That's not hunger. That's psychology.

Most of your spending doesn't start with a number , it starts with a feeling. A flicker of discomfort. A craving for ease, control, joy, escape. You think you're making a conscious choice, but beneath the surface, **your brain is pulling financial levers you're not even aware of**.

Welcome to the *real* story of your money.

This section - ***The Mind Under the Money-dives*** into the **hidden architecture of your spending behavior**. It's not about math or morals. It's about how we're all wired. And how that wiring gets exploited , by marketers, tech, social norms, even our own inner narratives.

You'll start by uncovering **the invisible influences behind every purchase**, how store layouts guide your steps, how colors and countdowns manipulate urgency, how social proof makes "everyone's doing it" feel like logic. You'll see how what feels like a personal choice is often a preloaded suggestion.

Then, we'll confront **the cost of comfort**. Why do we pay more for faster shipping, convenient apps, or premium experiences? Because our brains crave ease. And in a world that monetizes convenience, comfort has a price, and often, a hidden long-term cost.

Finally, we'll strip back the layers on **emotional spending** , the late-night retail therapy, the stress-fueled takeout, the celebration splurges. Emotions are powerful, and when they run unchecked, they don't just impact your mood, they hijack your wallet.

Here's the good news: none of this makes you weak, broken, or bad with money. It makes you human.
And once you see these patterns clearly, you can begin to interrupt them , to spend with awareness, not autopilot.

So pause for a moment and ask yourself: *What if your spending wasn't just about money… but about your mind?*
Let's find out.

CHAPTER 1: THE HIDDEN FORCES BEHIND EVERY PURCHASE

You probably think you're in charge when you shop. That when you choose the mid-priced bottle of wine, upgrade your phone "just in case," or grab that $14 moisturizer at checkout, you're making a rational, informed decision.

But what if I told you that many of those choices were made *before* you ever reached for your wallet?

Imagine walking through a grocery store. Soft lighting. Calming music. The scent of fresh bread wafting through the air. You came in for milk, but by the time you reach the register, your cart holds chocolate-covered almonds, a new reusable water bottle, and a two-for-one pasta deal. Did you *really* decide all that? Or did the store's design decide for you?

This chapter pulls back the curtain on the **invisible influencers embedded in your everyday environment, and in your brain.** These aren't just marketing tricks or bad habits. They're **deeply wired behavioral responses** that retailers, tech platforms, and even social media have learned to exploit, often better than we understand them ourselves.

We'll explore:

- **Decision fatigue**, and why your willpower runs on a timer

- How **priming and nudging** can steer you toward spending without you realizing it

- The danger of **scarcity traps**, like countdown timers and "Only 3 left!"

- Why **social proof** , like reviews or popularity badges , sways you even when you think it doesn't

- And the subtle power of the **anchoring effect**, where your brain compares prices based on irrelevant reference points

These aren't one-off glitches in your thinking, they're part of how the human brain operates in a noisy, fast-moving world. And unless you know what to look for, you'll keep spending on autopilot, convinced you're calling the shots.

But once you *see* these forces at play, you can start making financial decisions with clarity and control.

Ready to find out who's really pulling the strings when you shop?
Let's step behind the scenes.

1.1: Decision Fatigue

It's 8:30 p.m. You've worked a full day, fielded dozens of emails, sat through meetings, navigated traffic, and answered the age-old question: *What's for dinner?*
Now you're standing in the snack aisle, staring at granola bars. Organic? High-protein? Peanut-free? On sale? Before you know it, there's a family-sized pack of cookies in your cart , and you have no idea how it got there.

That's not just hunger. It's decision fatigue.

What Is Decision Fatigue, and Why Does It Matter?

Every decision you make, from what to wear to how to reply to a text, uses a tiny amount of your brain's mental fuel. Just like a phone

battery drains with every app you open, your willpower and decision-making ability decline throughout the day.
This phenomenon is called **decision fatigue**, and it's one of the most underestimated forces behind poor spending choices.

Coined by social psychologist Roy Baumeister, decision fatigue describes the deteriorating quality of decisions after a long session of decision-making. It's why judges are more likely to deny parole later in the day, why you're more likely to eat junk food after dinner, and why, when you're tired, you often default to what's easy rather than what's best.

In the financial world, this translates into *autopilot purchases, emotional spending, and surrendering to convenience.*

How Decision Fatigue Hijacks Your Wallet ?

Have you ever noticed that you're more likely to splurge after a tough day? Maybe you stop for takeout instead of cooking. Maybe you throw a few extras into your Amazon cart "just to feel better." This isn't a coincidence.
Mental fatigue drives us toward fast, feel-good, low-effort decisions , exactly the kind that lead to overspending.

Here's how it plays out in real life:

- **Grocery stores** place candy and snacks at checkout, not by accident , but because they know your brain is most depleted by the end of a shopping trip. You've made dozens of micro-decisions already. That Snickers bar? It's not indulgence , it's your brain waving the white flag.

- **Late-night online shopping** is another classic trap. After a long day of navigating stress, your decision-making filter is frayed. Suddenly, ads feel more persuasive. Reviews sound more convincing. Your future self will deal with the bill.

- **Subscription creep** often happens when we're too mentally taxed to evaluate value. It's easier to keep paying than to cancel, and the cost of "figuring it out later" seems worth it, until it isn't.

We like to think of our money choices as rational. But decision fatigue turns even the smartest spender into a short-term thinker. And the more tired we are, the more expensive those decisions become.

The Science Behind the Fog

The brain regions responsible for self-control, especially the **prefrontal cortex**, rely on glucose and rest. After repeated use, they get taxed, leaving you more reactive and less analytical. Studies show that even making simple decisions (like choosing between two shirts) drains mental resources. When those resources are low, your brain craves comfort and defaults to impulsive, emotionally driven behavior.

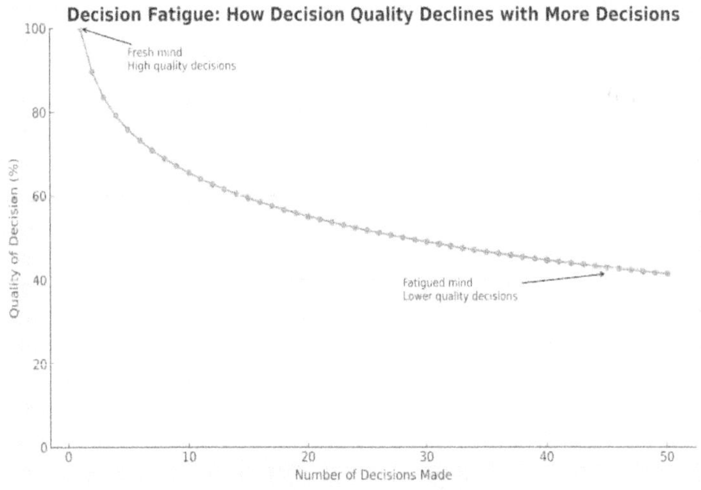

Figure 1.1 — The Decline of Decision Quality

This graph illustrates how the quality of our decisions drops as the number of decisions we make increases. It visually reinforces the concept that our mental energy, like a battery, depletes throughout the day, leaving us more prone to impulsive, emotionally driven financial behavior.

Baumeister's research also introduced the concept of **ego depletion**, the idea that willpower is finite. If you've resisted temptation all day , passed on cake at the office, answered difficult emails, avoided snapping at your boss , your brain starts looking for relief. And often, relief feels like a reward: *something new, something fun, something easy.*
Spending money is all three.

Real-World Scenario: The 9 p.m. Shopping Slip

Let's say Alex has a long commute home. By the time they arrive, they're hungry, mentally drained, and craving ease. A quick scroll on their phone turns into an Amazon spiral, workout gear, Bluetooth speakers, and a self-help book.
Total: $126.79.
Regret by morning? High.

That's not poor financial discipline. That's **neurological fatigue** in action. The brain simply didn't have enough gas left to pump the brakes.

How to Outsmart Decision Fatigue ?

The good news? You can't avoid decision fatigue, but you *can* design your life around it. Here are practical strategies to reduce its financial impact :

1. **Automate Wisely**:
   Use your mental energy for decisions that matter. Automate savings, bill payments, and investments so you're not negotiating with yourself every month.

2. **Front-Load Important Purchases**:
   Make high-impact financial decisions (budgeting, bill review,

big purchases) *early in the day* when your brain is fresh.

3. **Set Spending Boundaries in Advance**:
   Go to stores with a list. Set digital spending limits. Disable "Buy Now" buttons or one-click checkouts when possible , friction helps.

4. **Pre-Commit to Choices**:
   Meal prep, unsubscribe from marketing emails, and use subscription tracking tools to limit last-minute, energy-depleted choices.

5. **Take Breaks and Fuel Up**:
   Your brain needs glucose and rest to function. Hydrate. Eat balanced meals. Step away from your screen. Decision strength isn't just mental , it's physical.

6. **Use If-Then Planning**:
   Example: *If I feel tempted to buy something late at night, then I will save it to my wishlist and review it tomorrow.*
   This simple mental script can delay impulse and restore perspective.

Final Thought: Own Your Energy, Own Your Wallet

Decision fatigue doesn't make you weak, it makes you *human.* But ignoring it? That's what keeps you stuck in a cycle of financial frustration.

Recognizing when your brain is tired, and creating systems to support smarter decisions, is a radical act of self-leadership. It's not about more discipline; it's about designing smarter defaults.

So the next time you're about to click, swipe, or splurge at the end of a long day, ask yourself:
Is this what I truly want , or is this just my tired brain looking for a break?

Because the difference between reactive spending and intentional living often comes down to **when** , not just **what** , you choose.

Let's keep going. The brain behind your budget is just getting started.

1.2: Priming & Nudging

The Unseen Hands Guiding Your Wallet

Imagine walking into a bakery. The warm aroma of freshly baked bread envelops you, and soft classical music plays in the background. You hadn't planned on buying anything, yet you find yourself purchasing a croissant. This spontaneous decision isn't merely about hunger; it's a result of subtle psychological cues influencing your behavior.(renascence.io)

In the realm of consumer behavior, two powerful concepts, **priming** and **nudging**, play pivotal roles in shaping our purchasing decisions. Understanding these can empower you to make more intentional financial choices.

Priming: The Subtle Influencer

Priming refers to the psychological phenomenon where exposure to certain stimuli influences our subsequent thoughts, feelings, or actions, often without conscious awareness. These stimuli can be words, images, sounds, or even scents.(Verywell Mind)

For instance, a study demonstrated that playing French music in a wine store increased the sales of French wines, while German music led to higher sales of German wines. The music subtly influenced customers' choices without them realizing it.(Digital Marketing Agency - ALLDGT)

In retail environments, priming is ubiquitous:

- **Color Schemes**: Red is often used in sale signs to evoke urgency and excitement, prompting quicker purchasing decisions.(Helpful Professor)

- **Scent Marketing**: Retailers infuse stores with specific scents to create a pleasant atmosphere, encouraging customers to linger and spend more.

- **Product Placement**: Items placed at eye level or near checkout counters are more likely to be noticed and purchased.(Medium)

These subtle cues can significantly impact our spending habits, often leading us to make purchases we hadn't intended.

Nudging: Steering Choices Without Restricting Freedom

Nudging involves designing choices in a way that subtly steers people toward a particular decision without restricting their freedom to choose. Coined by behavioral economists Richard Thaler and Cass Sunstein, nudging leverages our cognitive biases to influence behavior in predictable ways.(The Decision Lab)

Common nudging techniques in consumer settings include:

- **Default Options**: Automatically enrolling employees in retirement savings plans, requiring them to opt-out if they choose not to participate.

- **Scarcity Messaging**: E-commerce sites often display messages like "Only 2 left in stock!" to create a sense of urgency.

- **Social Proof**: Highlighting best-selling items or customer reviews to influence purchasing decisions.

These strategies are designed to make certain choices more appealing or easier to select, often leading consumers toward decisions that benefit the business.

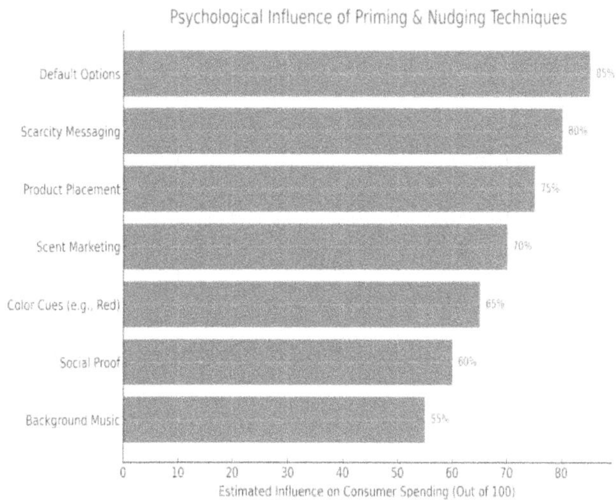

Figure 1.2- Influence of Priming & Nudging Techniques on Consumer Spending

This horizontal bar chart illustrates the estimated psychological influence of various priming and nudging techniques used in marketing and consumer environments. Techniques like default options (e.g., pre-selected choices in checkout), scarcity messaging ("Only 2 left!"), and social proof ("Trending now") have a stronger effect on consumer behavior than people often realize. This visual reinforces how these subtle strategies guide decisions subconsciously.

The Ethical Considerations

While priming and nudging can guide consumers toward beneficial choices, such as healthier eating or increased savings, they also raise ethical questions.

- **Autonomy**: Are consumers truly making free choices if they're being subtly influenced?

- **Transparency**: Should businesses disclose when they're using these techniques?

Ethicists argue that while nudging can be a powerful tool for positive change, it must be employed responsibly, ensuring that it respects individual autonomy and promotes genuine well-being.

Recognizing and Resisting Influence

To regain control over your spending habits, consider the following strategies:

- **Awareness**: Pay attention to environmental cues, music, scents, colors, that might be influencing your decisions.

- **Pause Before Purchasing**: Implement a waiting period before making non-essential purchases to determine if the desire persists.

- **Set Clear Intentions**: Shop with a list and stick to it, reducing susceptibility to in-store prompts.

- **Educate Yourself**: Understanding these psychological tactics can diminish their power over you.

Empowerment Through Awareness

Recognizing the subtle forces of priming and nudging in your daily life is the first step toward making more intentional financial decisions. By cultivating awareness, you can navigate consumer environments with greater autonomy, ensuring that your spending aligns with your true values and goals.

As you continue reading, consider how these invisible triggers have influenced your past purchases and how you can apply this knowledge to future financial choices.

1.3: Scarcity Traps

The Illusion of Now or Never

You're browsing your favorite online store, and a red banner catches your eye: "Only 2 left in stock!" Your heart skips a beat. You weren't planning to buy anything today, but suddenly, the idea of missing out feels unbearable. Within minutes, you've checked out.

This is the power of a scarcity trap.

Scarcity traps are psychological triggers that exploit our fear of missing out (FOMO) by creating the illusion that a product, opportunity, or deal is in short supply. The underlying principle is simple: when something appears rare, we assign it more value. This perception causes us to act fast, often impulsively, before we've had time to weigh the necessity or cost.

Retailers and marketers know this well. Limited-time offers, flash sales, and low-stock alerts are engineered to activate our primal instincts. And, the results? Billions in sales and countless unplanned purchases.

The Psychology of Scarcity: Why We React

Scarcity taps into one of our most deeply ingrained survival mechanisms. In ancient times, a limited food source meant act now or go hungry. Though modern society rarely requires such urgency, our brains haven't evolved past this primal reaction.

This urgency fuels impulsive spending. Rational decision-making takes a backseat as emotion takes the wheel. In a study by Kristina Durante at Rutgers Business School, participants exposed to scarcity cues exhibited more impulsive behavior and a preference for immediate rewards, even when delayed rewards were objectively better.

This is why during events like Black Friday, even the most disciplined consumers can find themselves in a frenzy, grabbing items they never intended to buy, simply because they fear missing out.

Three Forms of Scarcity Traps

Scarcity manifests in multiple ways, all of which exploit different aspects of consumer psychology:

1. **Quantity Scarcity**

    - Messages like "Only 3 left!" imply an item is nearly sold out. This drives urgency by suggesting that if you don't act now, you'll lose the opportunity forever. For example, Amazon uses real-time stock alerts that push consumers to check out quickly.

2. **Time Scarcity**

    - Flash sales, countdown clocks, and phrases like "Offer ends in 3 hours!" play on time scarcity. Brands like Zara and Shein regularly rotate inventory and promotions, making products seem fleeting and disposable. This cultivates urgency and rapid decision-making.

3. **Social Scarcity**

   - Labels such as "Popular item," "Trending now," or "Bestseller" create the illusion that everyone else wants the same item. These triggers herd behavior, where people follow perceived demand to avoid being left out. Think of concert tickets or limited-edition sneakers that sell out within minutes because "everyone" is buying them.

The Mental Shortcuts That Fuel Scarcity Buying

Scarcity increases perceived value, a principle backed by decades of behavioral research. In a classic 1975 study by Worchel, Lee, and Adewole, participants rated cookies from a jar with just two left as significantly more desirable than the same cookies in a full jar. The cookies didn't change; perception did.

Scarcity also plays directly into our cognitive bias of **loss aversion**, the idea that the pain of losing something is psychologically twice as powerful as the pleasure of gaining something. In scarcity-driven shopping, the fear of losing a deal outweighs the actual desire for the product.

This is why you might buy a second air fryer on sale even though the first one is still in the box.

After the High: Emotional Fallout of Scarcity Purchases

The momentary thrill of grabbing a "rare" deal often fades fast. In its place, many consumers experience buyer's remorse. That shirt from the flash sale? Never worn. The gadget labeled "Last chance to buy"? Sitting in a drawer.

These after-effects aren't just frustrating, they can create a cycle of financial stress and emotional dissatisfaction. Consumers may find themselves chasing deals not out of need, but from the addictive emotional high scarcity creates.

Breaking Free: How to Outsmart Scarcity Traps

The good news? Awareness is a powerful defense. Here are strategies to resist scarcity-driven impulses:

- **Pause and Reflect**: Before checking out, take a moment to ask: "Would I buy this if it weren't limited?" Often, the urgency fades with just a few minutes of distance.

- **Shop With Intention**: Make a list before you shop, online or in-store, and stick to it. If a deal pops up for something not on your list, skip it.

- **Assess Long-Term Value**: Ask yourself whether the item aligns with your goals or brings genuine value. "It's a great deal" is not a good enough reason.

- **Unsubscribe and Unfollow**: Reduce exposure to scarcity cues by unsubscribing from promotional emails or muting social media accounts that bombard you with flash sales.

- **Use the 24-Hour Rule**: If a deal tempts you, wait 24 hours. If you still want the item and it serves a real need, buy it. If not, you've avoided a trap.

A Better Way to Spend

Scarcity is a powerful force, and one of the most effective psychological levers used in modern marketing. It preys on our ancient instincts, pushes us to act without reflection, and often leaves us with things we never needed in the first place.

But there is power in mindfulness. Recognizing when urgency is artificial allows you to regain control. Spending becomes deliberate, not reactionary.

So the next time you see a "limited-time offer," take a breath. Ask yourself: Who really benefits from this urgency, me, or the seller?

Awareness is your strongest asset. Use it, and you'll spend with clarity instead of compulsion.

1.4: Social Proof

The Invisible Crowd That Shapes Your Spending

What Is Social Proof ?

Imagine you're in a new city, searching for a place to eat. You come across two restaurants: one bustling with patrons, the other nearly empty. Which one do you choose? Most people opt for the crowded spot, assuming its popularity signals quality. This instinct is known as **social proof**, the psychological phenomenon where we look to others' actions to guide our own behavior, especially in uncertain situations.

In the realm of consumer behavior, social proof influences our decisions daily. Whether it's choosing a product with numerous positive reviews or following a trend endorsed by influencers, we often rely on others' experiences to inform our choices.

The Psychology Behind Social Proof

Humans are inherently social creatures. From an evolutionary standpoint, aligning with group behavior increased our ancestors' chances of survival. This tendency persists today, manifesting as a desire for social validation and belonging.

Consider this: when faced with uncertainty, we often assume the group knows better. This "herd mentality" can lead us to adopt behaviors simply because others are doing so. Emotional triggers like the **fear of missing out (FOMO)** further amplify this effect, pushing us toward decisions that align with perceived social norms.

A vivid example is the phenomenon of laugh tracks in sitcoms. Even if we don't find a joke particularly funny, hearing others laugh prompts us to join in, reinforcing the idea that the content is humorous.

Social Proof in the Digital Age

The advent of the internet and social media has magnified the impact of social proof. Online platforms provide immediate access to others' opinions, making it easier than ever to gauge public sentiment.

- **Online Reviews**: Before making a purchase, many consumers consult reviews on platforms like Amazon or Yelp. A product with numerous positive reviews is more likely to be chosen over one with few or negative feedback.

- **Influencer Endorsements**: Social media influencers wield significant power in shaping consumer preferences. Their endorsements can drive massive sales, as followers often perceive them as trusted sources.

- **Trending Hashtags and Viral Content**: Content that gains traction online often benefits from the bandwagon effect. As more people engage with a trend, others follow suit, further amplifying its reach.

Algorithms on platforms like Instagram and TikTok also play a role by promoting content that garners high engagement, creating a feedback loop where popular content becomes even more visible.

Real-World Examples of Social Proof

The Dark Side of Social Proof

While social proof can guide us toward beneficial decisions, it also has pitfalls.

- **Impulse Buying**: The desire to conform can lead to unnecessary purchases. Seeing a product labeled as "bestseller" might prompt a buy, even if it's not needed.

- **Scams and Misinformation**: Fraudulent schemes often exploit social proof by fabricating testimonials or inflating follower counts to appear legitimate.

- **Overreliance on Popular Opinion**: Blindly following trends can stifle individuality and lead to choices that don't align with personal values or needs.

Navigating Social Proof Wisely

To harness the benefits of social proof without falling prey to its downsides:

- **Pause and Reflect**: Before making a purchase influenced by popularity, ask yourself if it aligns with your genuine needs.

- **Seek Diverse Opinions**: Don't rely solely on star ratings. Read a range of reviews to get a comprehensive understanding.

- **Be Skeptical of Hype**: Just because something is trending doesn't mean it's right for you. Evaluate products and services based on their merits, not just their popularity.

- **Limit Social Media Exposure**: Reducing time spent on platforms can decrease susceptibility to trends driven by influencers.

Empowering Your Financial Decisions

Social proof is a powerful force in shaping our behaviors and choices. By understanding its mechanisms, you can make more informed decisions that align with your values and financial goals.

Reflective Questions:

1. Can you recall a recent purchase influenced by others' opinions or behaviors? Was it a wise decision?
2. How do you differentiate between genuine recommendations and marketing tactics designed to exploit social proof?
3. What strategies can you implement to ensure your spending aligns with personal needs rather than societal pressures?

By cultivating awareness and critical thinking, you can navigate the complexities of consumer behavior and make choices that truly serve your best interests.

1.5: Anchoring Effect

The Invisible Starting Point That Shapes Every Price You See

1. Introduction to the Anchoring Effect

Imagine walking into a store and seeing a designer jacket priced at $1,200. You'd probably raise an eyebrow. But then you see a similar-looking jacket for $300. Suddenly, $300 feels like a bargain, even if you had no intention of spending that much in the first place. This is the anchoring effect in action.

The **anchoring effect** refers to our tendency to rely heavily on the first piece of information we encounter, the "**anchor**", when making decisions. In consumer psychology, that anchor often sets the baseline for how we perceive value. Once a price is planted in our minds, all subsequent prices are judged relative to it, even if the original number is arbitrary or inflated.

This mental shortcut influences everyday purchasing decisions more than most people realize. Whether you're choosing a smartphone, negotiating a salary, or booking a flight, chances are you're being unconsciously nudged by an anchor.

2. The Psychology Behind Anchoring

Our brains crave efficiency. We're constantly bombarded with decisions, so our cognitive systems use mental shortcuts, also known as heuristics, to reduce the burden. Anchoring is one of those shortcuts.

Pioneering psychologists **Daniel Kahneman and Amos Tversky** found that when people are presented with a number (even a random one), it affects their subsequent judgments. In one experiment, participants spun a wheel rigged to land on either 10 or 65. When asked to guess the percentage of African countries in the United Nations, those who saw "10" guessed significantly lower than those who saw "65." The initial number anchored their thinking, even though it was clearly irrelevant.

Emotionally, anchoring taps into our perception of value and fairness. A high anchor can make us feel like we're getting a deal when we pay less, even if that lower price is still above market value. It creates a psychological frame that colors our decision, much like a tinted lens distorts color.

Think of anchoring like your GPS giving you a route: even if it's not the best one, you're more likely to follow it unless you pause to assess alternatives.

3. Anchoring in Everyday Spending

Anchors are everywhere, especially in retail. Consider the classic "Was $100, now only $49.99" tag. The original price is the anchor, making $49.99 look irresistible. But was the product ever really worth $100?

In fashion, luxury brands set high anchor prices. A $2,000 handbag from a designer brand makes a $500 handbag seem modest by comparison, even though $500 is still a significant expense. The luxury item exists, in part, to shape your perception of the other options.

Negotiations are also prime ground for anchoring. In real estate, a home listed at $750,000 anchors your expectations, even if comparable homes in the neighborhood sell for $650,000. The same goes for car dealerships and salary talks, the initial number shapes the conversation.

In travel, airlines often list inflated "original" prices for tickets and then show limited-time discounts. That $199 flight looks amazing compared to the "regular" $349, regardless of whether anyone actually pays the regular fare.

4. The Anchoring Effect in the Digital Age

Anchoring has become even more potent in the age of e-commerce and digital marketing. Algorithms are trained to show you anchors that influence behavior.

- **Dynamic Pricing**: Airlines, hotel booking sites, and ride-share apps use algorithms to set fluctuating prices. By showing you a high anchor first ("average fare is $400"), they make a lower price look appealing, even if that price has been manipulated.

- **"Compare At" Pricing**: Online retailers love using strike-through prices to create anchors. Seeing "$149" crossed out next to "$79" conditions your mind to believe you're saving big.

- **Subscription Models**: Companies often present multiple tiers, Basic, Standard, and Premium, with the highest tier priced exorbitantly to make the middle option look more reasonable. This strategy, called **price bracketing**, uses the high anchor to guide you toward their preferred choice.

Even social proof plays a role. Seeing "Most Popular Plan" under a mid-tier subscription is another way to nudge you using anchoring, layered with crowd influence.

5. The Dark Side of Anchoring

Anchoring can lead to financially harmful choices:

- **Overpaying**: When a high anchor sets your expectation, you may pay more than something is worth simply because it feels cheaper than the original number.

- **False Deals**: Retailers inflate original prices just to mark them down. That 70% off deal might still be more expensive than comparable products elsewhere.

- **Anchored Expectations**: Once your mind latches onto a price or value, it's hard to adjust—even when new information contradicts it. This rigidity can trap you into poor budgeting or bad investment decisions.

Companies intentionally exploit anchoring to manipulate perceptions. The more emotionally charged or urgent the decision (e.g., "limited time offer"), the more susceptible you become.

6. How to Overcome the Anchoring Effect ?

Awareness is the first line of defense. Once you know you're being anchored, you can consciously reframe your decisions.

Here's how:

- **Do Your Own Research**: Compare prices across different retailers and platforms. Don't rely on the first number you see.

- **Set Internal Anchors**: Before shopping, decide what you're willing to pay. Create your own mental reference points based on needs and budget, not external suggestions.

- **Take a Pause**: Delay purchases, especially during sales. Time helps reduce the emotional pull of anchors.

- **Mind the Middle Option**: In pricing models with three tiers, be cautious of how your choice is being guided. Middle isn't always best, it's just designed to appear that way.

7. Conclusion and Reflection

Anchors are powerful not because they're always accurate, but because they frame our perception of what's acceptable or reasonable. In the world of spending, that first price you see often becomes the lens through which all other values are judged.

But you're not powerless. By learning to spot anchors and slow down your decision-making, you can reclaim control over your financial habits.

Ask yourself:

- What anchors have influenced your recent spending decisions?

- How might your financial choices change if you set your own anchors before shopping?

Understanding the anchoring effect is like learning to spot the magician's trick, it won't make the illusion disappear, but it will give you the power not to fall for it.

1.6: The Toolbox- 3 Questions That Transform How You Spend

The 3-Question Trigger Audit

Every spending decision you make is influenced by something deeper than price tags or product specs. It's often shaped by invisible psychological triggers, emotions, social cues, internal narratives, and environmental nudges. Marketers have long studied how to exploit these hidden levers. The question is: have *you* studied how to spot them?

The **3-Question Trigger Audit** is a simple but powerful tool designed to put you back in the driver's seat of your financial decisions. With just three questions, it helps you pause, examine your motivations, and align your spending with your true goals and values.

1. Why Do I Want This?

This question peels back the curtain on your initial desire. Is it rooted in **emotion**, or is it grounded in a **practical** need?

We often spend money not because we need something, but because we're chasing a feeling, relief from stress, a hit of excitement, a moment of control, or a sense of belonging.

Emotional Triggers:

- Boredom: "I need a pick-me-up, maybe a new gadget will help."
- Social Comparison: "Everyone's wearing this brand—I don't want to feel left out."

- Stress: "I've had a hard week. I deserve this."

Practical Triggers:

- Functionality: "I need a durable laptop for my job."
- Replacement: "My shoes are worn out and uncomfortable."
- Planning: "I've budgeted for this, and it aligns with my needs."

Knowing whether your spending is emotionally or practically motivated helps you make a conscious choice instead of a reactive one.

2. How Will I Feel About This in a Week, a Month, or a Year?

This is your time machine question.

When we shop, we tend to zoom in on *how we feel now*. Marketers want you to ride that emotional high, the dopamine hit of a flash sale, the thrill of one-click ordering, the rush of having something new. But what about *later*?

Ask yourself:

- Will this item still feel exciting a week from now?
- Will I still think it was worth the money in a month?
- Will it contribute to or detract from my long-term goals a year from now?

Our brains are wired for short-term rewards, but financial health is built on long-term thinking. This question helps recalibrate your lens from *now* to *next*.

3. Does This Align With My Financial Goals or Values?

This final question brings your decision back to *you*, your goals, your values, your vision of success.

Every dollar you spend is a vote for the kind of life you want. So ask:

- Does this purchase move me closer to what matters, or pull me further away?
- Is this aligned with my budget, or is it a detour?
- Am I spending with intention, or reacting to emotion or external pressure?

Intentional spending is not about restriction. It's about direction.

Putting It Into Practice

Imagine you're about to buy a $300 designer jacket you saw on social media.

- **Why do I want this?** "Because it's trending and makes me feel stylish." (Emotional trigger)
- **How will I feel in a month?** "Probably less excited, especially if I see something newer."
- **Does this align with my goals?** "No. I'm trying to pay down credit card debt."

Just three questions, and suddenly, you've stepped out of autopilot and into self-awareness.

Try this audit before your next purchase. Keep it on your phone. Bookmark it. Practice it. Over time, it becomes a habit, one that can fundamentally reshape your relationship with money.

Case Study: IKEA & Your Lizard Brain

Walk into any IKEA store and you're immediately immersed in a carefully curated environment, room after room of stylish, functional furniture, softly lit spaces, and the warm aroma of cinnamon buns. You came in for a desk lamp. You leave with candles, a storage unit, a set of wine glasses, and a new sense of domestic aspiration.

That wasn't accidental. It was **instinctual**; your **lizard brain** took the wheel.

What Is the Lizard Brain?

The "lizard brain" is a nickname for the limbic system—the oldest part of your brain, responsible for instinct, survival, and emotion. It doesn't think critically or plan ahead. It responds.

When activated, the lizard brain doesn't ask, *"Is this within budget?"* It asks, *"Do I want this now?"*

Marketers know this, and IKEA has perfected the art of tapping into it.

1. The Maze-Like Store Layout

IKEA's famous one-way, winding layout isn't just about aesthetics. It's a **psychological funnel**.

By guiding customers through every department in a linear path, IKEA turns shopping into a journey. You're not just browsing, you're *exploring*, which taps into our brain's reward system. Each new section brings novelty, discovery, and opportunity, perfect fuel for the lizard brain's love of unpredictability.

This layout also removes friction: instead of asking, *"Do I need this?"* you're primed to think, *"Where could I put this?"*

2. Low Prices + Emotional Triggers

IKEA products are often surprisingly affordable. A chair for $35. A set of plates for $9. A shelf for under $50. These low prices anchor the idea that you're getting **value**, which disarms the rational part of your brain.

But here's where it gets clever: these items are displayed in cozy, aspirational spaces. That $35 chair? It's not just a chair, it's part of a minimalist reading nook in a Parisian-inspired studio. The setting isn't selling furniture; it's selling a *feeling.*

The lizard brain eats this up. It connects the product with the emotion: *If I buy this, I'll feel like that.*

3. The IKEA Effect

There's a deeper layer of psychology at play: what researchers call the **IKEA Effect**.

In a 2011 study by Dan Ariely and colleagues, participants placed a significantly higher value on items they assembled themselves compared to pre-made equivalents. Why? Because effort equals ownership.

When you assemble a bookshelf, you're not just building furniture, you're investing emotional labor. That sense of accomplishment activates your brain's reward centers and increases the perceived value of the item.

This not only makes you love the item more, it makes you more likely to justify the purchase, keep it longer, and buy again.

Jamie's IKEA Journey

Let's meet Jamie. She walks into IKEA for a coffee table. Ninety minutes later, she's hauling a cart filled with dishware, plant pots, picture frames, and a rug. She even picked up a storage unit, "just in case."

What happened?

Her lizard brain was activated by:

- The thrill of the maze-like layout
- The allure of low prices
- The emotional pull of beautifully staged rooms
- The anticipated satisfaction of assembling something herself

By the time Jamie left the store, the decision-making part of her brain had long been overruled by instincts and emotion.

Reflect and Reclaim Control

IKEA's strategy is brilliant, and effective. But now that you know what's happening behind the scenes, you can navigate your next trip with more awareness.

Ask yourself:

- Am I reacting to a feeling or responding with intention?
- Is this item solving a problem, or am I just chasing a mood?
- Is my lizard brain doing the shopping , or am I?

The more you understand your brain's default settings, the better equipped you are to override them. And the more control you have over your spending, not just at IKEA, but everywhere.

Chapter 2: The Cost of Comfort Loops

Have you ever stopped to calculate how much you spend in a month on things designed to make life easier? The extra fee for same-day delivery. The automatic refill of your favorite skincare product. The streaming platforms you forgot you subscribed to, until they quietly debited your account again last Tuesday.

These aren't reckless splurges or financial emergencies. They're something subtler, sneakier. They're comfort loops.

A *comfort loop* is a cycle of behavior where convenience, routine, and emotional relief reinforce each other, until they become automatic. It starts with a small reward: a latte that brightens a tough morning, a subscription box that sparks joy on your doorstep, or an app that promises fewer errands and more free time. Over time, these purchases hardwire themselves into your daily rhythm, offering quick hits of ease and satisfaction in exchange for something less obvious: your long-term financial clarity.

The problem isn't comfort itself. It's the cost of not noticing how often we trade money for momentary relief, and how those small trades stack up. Comfort loops rarely feel like "spending problems." They feel like normal life. Which is why they're so powerful, and so financially dangerous.

Think about it: How many of your spending habits today are driven not by conscious choice, but by routine? How many align with who you think you are, or who you want to be seen as? And how many quietly accumulate month after month, untouched, because they're tucked behind a login or buried in a credit card statement?

In this chapter, we'll break down the invisible architecture behind these loops:

- In **Habit Loop Theory**, we'll explore how your brain forms spending routines through a simple formula: cue, routine, reward. You'll learn why that familiar "treat yourself" impulse isn't random, it's rehearsed.

- In **Identity Spending**, we'll look at how your purchases reflect (and often shape) who you believe you are. Whether it's the tools of a minimalist or the gadgets of a productivity junkie, your financial behavior often mirrors your internal story.

- And in **Subscription Drift**, we'll investigate the slow leak of recurring charges that go unnoticed. From music platforms to meditation apps, we'll show how convenience can quietly become clutter, both digitally and financially.

This chapter isn't about shaming your morning coffee or telling you to cancel everything that makes life a little easier. It's about pressing pause, so you can ask: *Am I spending out of intention or inertia?*

As you read on, stay curious. Notice your own comfort loops. You may discover that the path to financial freedom isn't paved with restriction, it's revealed through awareness.

What are your habits really costing you, and what could you gain by seeing them clearly?

2.1: Habit Loop Theory

Have you ever found yourself pulling into the drive-thru of your favorite coffee shop without even thinking? Maybe you weren't particularly tired, and you weren't craving caffeine. Yet there you were, ordering the same drink you always do. That, right there, is the power of a habit loop in action.

Understanding the Habit Loop

The habit loop is a simple yet powerful psychological model that explains how habits form and why they stick. It consists of three parts: the **cue**, the **routine**, and the **reward**.

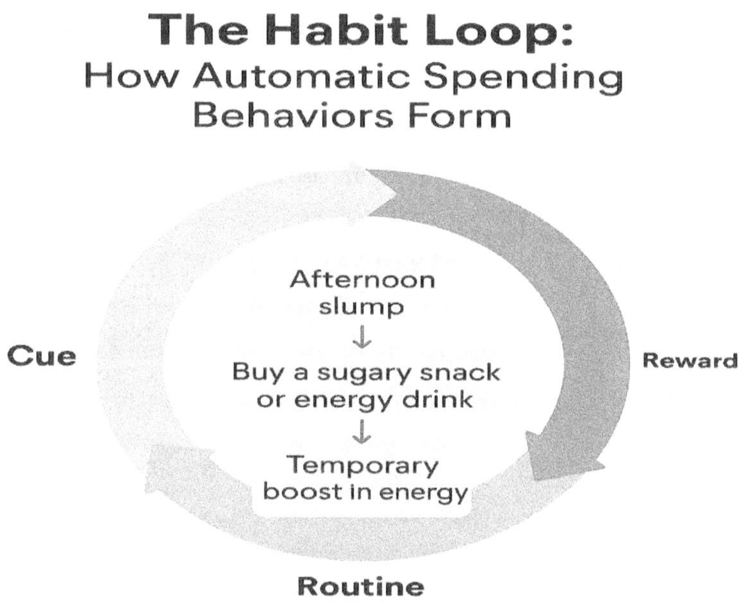

Figure 1:
Habits follow a predictable neurological pattern: cue, routine, reward. Over time, these loops become automatic, guiding spending decisions with little conscious thought.

Let's break it down:

- **Cue:** This is the trigger that initiates the behavior. It could be a time of day, an emotional state, or something in your environment.

- **Routine:** The behavior itself, what you do in response to the cue.

- **Reward:** The benefit you get from performing the routine. It satisfies a craving or delivers pleasure, even if momentary.

Take this everyday example: You drive by your usual coffee shop on your way to work (cue). Without much thought, you pull in and order a latte (routine). You sip it, feel a little more energized, and enjoy the comfort of your morning ritual (reward). This loop, repeated over days, becomes a default behavior, so automatic you hardly notice it.

The Brain and Habit Formation

Why are habits so persistent? The answer lies in your brain. Specifically, the **basal ganglia**, the part of your brain responsible for storing routines and patterns, helps automate tasks to conserve mental energy.

Habits allow the brain to operate efficiently, freeing up space for other tasks. But this efficiency has a downside: once a habit loop is established, your brain stops fully participating in the decision-making process. The behavior becomes nearly automatic, especially if the cue and reward remain consistent.

This is why it's so easy to form spending habits without realizing it. Every time you respond to a familiar cue with a spending action and get a reward, even a small one, you deepen the loop.

Habit Loops and Spending Behavior

Now let's bring this closer to home: your wallet. Spending behaviors often follow well-worn habit loops, even if we believe we're making thoughtful choices.

- **Impulse Buys Triggered by Emotions:** You're stressed after a long day (cue), so you browse an online store (routine) and feel a burst of pleasure when you buy something new reward).

- **Daily Spending Rituals:** You always grab lunch from the same cafe (routine) when the clock hits noon (cue), because it feels good to take a break and treat yourself (reward).

- **Marketing as Cue Manipulation:** Retailers are experts at tapping into our habit loops. That "limited-time offer" or app notification is designed to act as a cue, prompting you to take action quickly and trigger a purchase before you even have time to reflect.

Each action may seem small, but over time, these loops can add up to significant financial leakage.

Comfort Loops: Feel-Good Spending That Adds Up

This brings us to the idea of **comfort loops**. These are habit loops specifically tied to routines that offer short-term comfort or convenience at a long-term cost.

Let's say you subscribe to three different streaming platforms, a meal kit delivery service, and a subscription box for your pet. Each was initially exciting, and each provides a sense of ease or pleasure (reward). But over time, you stop questioning whether you're still using all of them (routine), because their automated nature keeps them running in the background (cue: a recurring bill).

Comfort loops feel good at the moment, but they often come with financial consequences that are easy to ignore. They're comforting routines that start to operate on autopilot, quietly draining your resources.

Breaking the Habit Loop

The good news? Habit loops are not destiny. Once you understand how they work, you can begin to disrupt the cycle. Here's how:

1. Recognize the Cue

The first step is awareness. Start by tracking your spending habits for a week. Ask yourself: What triggers each purchase? Is it a time of day, a mood, or a specific place or notification? Noticing these patterns can help you bring automatic behavior into conscious awareness.

2. Modify the Routine

Next, experiment with changing your routine. If your cue is stress and your routine is shopping online, try replacing it with something that still soothes you, like journaling, meditating, or calling a friend. The goal isn't to remove comfort; it's to replace it with a healthier habit that doesn't rely on spending.

3. Reframe the Reward

Finally, redefine what you find rewarding. If you're trying to break your daily coffee shop habit, don't just cut it out. Replace it with a reward that gives you similar pleasure or satisfaction—like brewing your favorite beans at home and enjoying them in a cozy spot with music or a podcast.

A Real-Life Example: Rewriting the Loop

Let's walk through a common scenario:

- **Cue:** You feel overwhelmed after work.

- **Routine:** You pull out your phone and start browsing your favorite shopping app. You buy a new gadget or piece of clothing.

- **Reward:** You feel a short-lived sense of excitement or control.

To break this loop:

- **Recognize the cue:** You realize that stress is your trigger.

- **Replace the routine:** Instead of opening the app, you take a walk, do a short breathing exercise, or write in a journal.

- **Reframe the reward:** You shift your focus to feeling calm and clear-headed, rather than temporarily thrilled.

Over time, repeating this new loop builds a more sustainable and financially healthy habit.

Conclusion: Awareness is the First Step

Habits are powerful because they operate silently, below the surface of our awareness. But when you bring light to them, when you pause to examine the cues, routines, and rewards driving your spending behaviors, you regain control.

The purpose of understanding the habit loop isn't to remove all comfort or to create guilt around spending. It's to empower you with the tools to make deliberate choices. When you're aware of your loops, you can rewrite them in ways that align with your values and financial goals.

So ask yourself:

What spending habits are part of your daily comfort loops, and how might you rewrite them to better align with your financial goals?
What cues trigger your most frequent purchases, and how can you disrupt the cycle?

Your brain is designed for habits. Now, it's time to design them in your favor.

2.2: Identity Spending

Have you ever bought something not because you needed it, but because it just felt like *you*? Maybe it was a sleek leather notebook that made you feel like the kind of person who journals daily. Or perhaps it was the latest fitness tracker, not because your old one was broken, but because it fit your image of someone who takes their health seriously. These purchases are more than transactions, they're statements. And they fall into a powerful and often unconscious behavioral pattern called **identity spending**.

What Is Identity Spending?

Identity spending happens when we use money to reinforce or project our self-image. We don't just buy clothes, gadgets, or services for their function, we buy them because they say something about who we are, or who we want to be. Sometimes, the message is to ourselves: *I'm a responsible adult, I deserve this.* Other times, it's for others: *See, I'm successful, stylish, fit, cultured, eco-conscious.*

This isn't always a bad thing. Money is one of the tools we use to express identity. But when this behavior becomes automatic, woven into our comfort loops, it can quietly drive overspending and disconnect our financial behavior from our actual needs or goals.

Why Identity Shapes Spending

From a psychological perspective, identity is central to how we navigate the world. It's the internal compass that guides our decisions, from career choices to how we decorate our homes. Psychologist Erik Erikson described identity as a sense of continuity within ourselves, who we believe we are and how we fit into society.

Spending becomes a key part of this process because it offers quick, tangible ways to confirm or reshape that identity. It taps into what behavioral scientists call *symbolic consumption*, the idea that we consume not just for utility, but to symbolize something larger.

There's also a social layer. Social comparison theory tells us we evaluate ourselves in part by comparing to others. So, when your friend upgrades to the latest phone or starts wearing high-end athletic gear, it's easy to feel the pull to do the same. This isn't just about keeping up with the Joneses, it's about maintaining your place in a social narrative that feels familiar, secure, and validating.

And don't forget about Maslow. His hierarchy of needs puts *esteem* and *self-actualization* near the top, needs that are often addressed through identity-affirming actions. For many, buying something that aligns with their self-image is a shortcut to feeling confident, competent, or connected.

What Identity Spending Looks Like ?

Let's look at a few real-world examples. If you recognize yourself in any of these, you're not alone.

- **Luxury Spending**: Buying high-end brands to project success or reward yourself after a stressful week. "I've worked hard, I deserve a little luxury," you might say, even if it strains your credit card.

- **Wellness and Fitness Purchases**: You spend hundreds on supplements, athleisure wear, or boutique gym classes, not because your health demands it, but because it aligns with how you see yourself (or want to be seen): someone who takes their well-being seriously.

- **Fashion for Self-Expression**: Dressing to reflect individuality or belonging to a subculture. Whether you lean toward streetwear, minimalism, or vintage chic, clothing becomes a costume for identity performance.

- **Green Consumerism**: Buying eco-friendly products as a way of expressing values around sustainability. These purchases feel virtuous and affirm your place in a socially responsible identity, even if they're more expensive or redundant.

None of these spending choices are inherently wrong. In fact, they often bring a sense of empowerment. But the problem arises when they slip into unconscious comfort loops, when they become defaults we don't question.

Identity Spending: The Loop Between Self-Image and Spending Habits

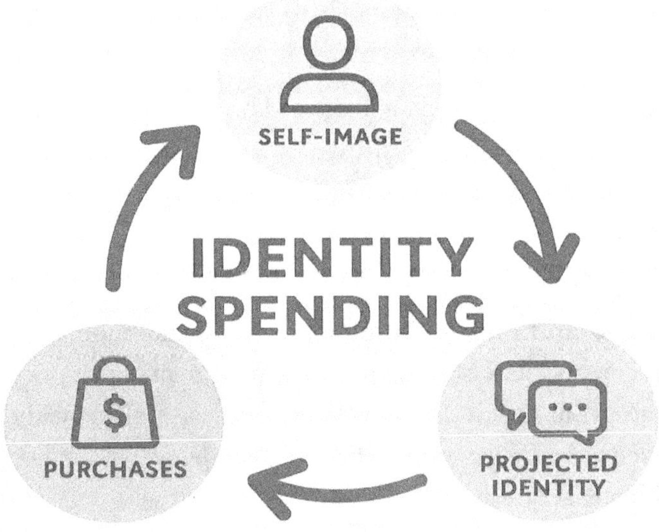

Figure 2.2: *This diagram illustrates how self-image influences spending behavior through a repeating loop: identity triggers lead to purchases that reinforce a desired*

identity, providing temporary emotional rewards that feed back into one's self-concept.

The Cost of Identity Comfort Loops

Comfort loops, as discussed earlier in this chapter, are habits tied to short-term emotional comfort. Identity spending can easily become one of these loops. When you're feeling unsure of yourself, insecure, or socially off-balance, reinforcing your identity through spending feels good. It brings a sense of familiarity, even safety.

But here's the catch: these comfort loops can mask real financial harm. You may accumulate unused subscription services that you "should" use because they align with your identity, like an online learning platform or a gourmet meal kit. Or you justify high-cost purchases with the narrative that it's "just who you are," even if your bank account tells a different story.

This pattern becomes especially risky when identity is tied to *external validation.* That is, when the image you're trying to maintain is more about how others see you than what truly fulfills you. When your spending is guided by the desire to be seen a certain way rather than to *be* a certain way, it's easy to fall into a cycle of financial self-sabotage.

How to Break Free from Identity-Based Spending ?

The good news? You don't have to give up expressing yourself through your purchases. But it's worth asking: *Am I spending in alignment with who I really am, or who I think I'm supposed to be?*

Here are a few ways to regain control:

1. Define Your Core Values
Start by identifying what truly matters to you. Is it creativity? Freedom? Family? Sustainability? Once you have clarity on your values, you can better evaluate whether your spending aligns with them, or just imitates them.

2. Track Your Identity Triggers

Just like you can track habit cues, you can track identity triggers. Notice when you feel the urge to buy something that reinforces a certain image. What prompted it? A social media post? A stressful event? Take a moment to pause and ask, *Is this really about the item, or about what it says about me?*

3. Practice Mindful Buying

Before each purchase, try the "why test." Ask yourself:

- Why am I buying this?
- What need am I trying to meet, utility or identity?
- Will this item still matter to me in a month?

4. Build Identity Without Buying

Identity doesn't have to be bought. If you see yourself as a creative person, write or draw instead of buying new supplies. If health is core to you, go for a walk or stretch at home instead of chasing the latest gear. Reinforce your identity through action, not accumulation.

5. Redefine Reward

Sometimes, the biggest reward isn't the thing you buy, it's the feeling it gives you. So, ask: Can I get that feeling in a different way? If buying a new outfit makes you feel confident, what else could give you that same sense of self-assurance?

Closing Thoughts

Identity spending is deeply human. We all want to feel seen, understood, and aligned with who we believe we are. But when that desire becomes tethered to automatic spending habits, it can quietly lead us away from financial health and self-awareness.

By becoming more mindful of your identity-driven purchases, you can begin to rewrite the script. You can still express who you are, just with more intention and less financial strain.

So the next time you reach for your wallet, pause and ask: *Is this purchase about what I need, or who I think I need to be?*

2.3: Subscription Drift

Picture this: It's the end of the month, and you're reviewing your bank statement. A few dollars here, ten bucks there, charges from streaming platforms, cloud storage, fitness apps, maybe a meditation app you downloaded in January during a wellness kick. You barely notice them. But together, they quietly eat away at your finances. This is *subscription drift* in action.

What Is Subscription Drift?

Subscription drift refers to the gradual accumulation of recurring payments for services you rarely use, or completely forget you have. These aren't extravagant purchases. In fact, their affordability is exactly what makes them so dangerous. A $4.99 charge doesn't raise alarms. But $4.99 times 10 unused services over a year? That's hundreds of dollars leaking from your budget.

In the age of the subscription economy, this drift is everywhere. We subscribe to entertainment (Netflix, Hulu, Spotify), fitness (Peloton, gym memberships), productivity (Google Drive, Evernote), and even groceries (meal kits, coffee clubs). Subscriptions offer convenience and consistency, two powerful comforts. But when we stop paying attention, that comfort becomes a trap. It forms a *comfort loop*, where the ease of recurring services overrides our rational assessment of their actual value.

Why Subscriptions Are So Sticky

The stickiness of subscriptions isn't accidental, it's psychological. They're engineered to be "set-it-and-forget-it" services, which is exactly what most of us do. You sign up once, feel the benefit for a while, and then... forget. Your credit card keeps getting charged, but the service fades into the background.

This behavior is rooted in several psychological biases:

- **Loss aversion**: We fear giving something up, even if we don't use it. Canceling a subscription feels like losing access, even if we haven't logged in for months.

- **Mental accounting**: We treat recurring small charges as minor expenses, barely noticeable in the moment. But they add up significantly over time.

- **Optimism bias**: We overestimate our future intentions. "I'll use that language app next month." "I'll get back to yoga soon." This makes us hold on to subscriptions we intend to use but realistically won't.

- **Anchoring bias**: Free trials lure us in with a low barrier to entry, anchoring our perception of value. Once the trial ends, many of us forget to cancel—even if the service no longer fits our needs.

Businesses know all this. That's why subscriptions often default to **auto-renewal**, **bundling**, and **tiered pricing**. They're designed not just to serve us, but to maximize how long we *stay subscribed*, whether or not we're actively engaged.

Real-Life Examples of Subscription Drift

Let's bring this to life:

- **Streaming inertia**: You subscribed to Disney+ to watch *The Mandalorian.* The season ended, but your subscription didn't. Six months later, you're still paying, even though you haven't logged in.

- **Fitness fade**: You joined a gym in January. By March, your visits tapered off—but the $49 monthly fee continues. "Maybe next week," you tell yourself.

- **Forgotten apps**: That productivity tool you downloaded last year? It bills annually, and you only realize it when the charge appears out of nowhere. Too late to cancel. Again.

Each of these examples may seem minor. But added together, they can become a slow financial leak, one that goes unnoticed until you take a hard look at your spending patterns.

The Subscription Drift Trap: How Small Charges Add Up Over Time

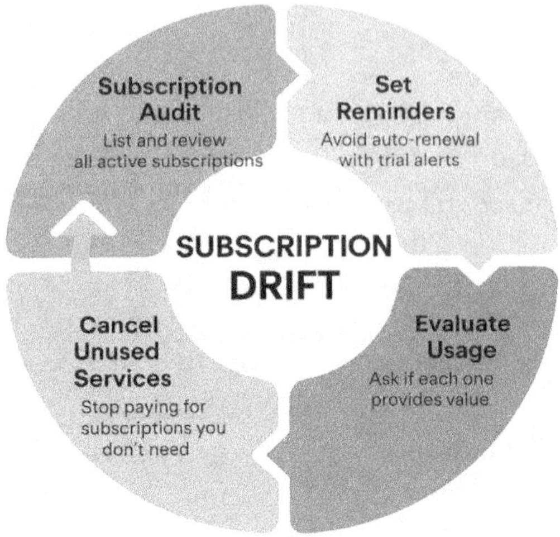

***Figure 2.3**: This infographic visually illustrates how minor recurring subscription costs, often perceived as insignificant, accumulate over months and years. It highlights the types of common subscriptions, the psychological traps that sustain them, and the cumulative financial impact if left unchecked.*

Comfort Loops and Subscription Drift

Subscription drift is a textbook example of a comfort loop. These services give us a *sense* of control, productivity, or identity, even if we're not actively using them. A fitness app on your phone makes you feel like you're a person who works out. A premium news subscription makes you feel informed. A cloud backup service makes you feel organized.

This illusion of value keeps us subscribed. We confuse *potential* utility with *actual* use. And because subscriptions are passive-they renew automatically-we're rarely forced to reevaluate them.

The longer the comfort loop goes unchallenged, the deeper it gets. We get used to seeing those charges and stop questioning them. It becomes "just part of the budget," even if it doesn't serve a meaningful role in our lives anymore.

How to Escape Subscription Drift ?

The good news is you can take back control. Breaking free from subscription drift isn't about eliminating every recurring expense. It's about *intentionality*. Here's how to start:

1. Conduct a Subscription Audit

Sit down with your bank and credit card statements. List every recurring charge, monthly, quarterly, annually. Ask yourself:

- How often do I actually use this?
- Does this bring me consistent value?
- Would I miss it if I canceled today?

You might be surprised by what you find.

2. Cancel What You Don't Use

This seems obvious, but it's often the hardest step. That's because canceling sometimes means letting go of a version of yourself you're *aspiring* to be, whether that's a reader, a yogi, a language learner, or a productivity guru.

Let go of the guilt. Your financial health matters more than the illusion of who you might be "someday."

3. Use Subscription Management Tools

Apps like Truebill, Rocket Money, or Mint can help track, categorize, and even cancel subscriptions. They bring awareness to the services silently siphoning your money.

4. Set Reminders for Trial Periods

If you're trying a new service, set a calendar reminder a few days before the trial ends. This gives you space to evaluate before the billing kicks in.

5. Adopt a Pay-As-You-Go Mindset

You don't need to commit to ongoing charges to enjoy a service. Many platforms now offer day passes, rental options, or à la carte pricing. Before subscribing, ask: *Is there a one-time or lower-commitment option that meets my needs?*

6. Align Spending With Values

Not every subscription is wasteful. Some bring joy, learning, or productivity. The key is alignment. Ask yourself: *Does this subscription reflect what I actually value, or is it just a holdover from an old habit?*

Wrapping It All Together

Subscription drift doesn't happen overnight. It's a slow, silent accumulation of services that feel harmless individually but create financial drag collectively. The comfort they offer is often just that, a *feeling*, not a function.

But you're not stuck. Awareness is the first step toward reclaiming control. When you begin to see subscriptions as choices rather than background noise, you create space for intentional, value-based spending.

So next time you spot that monthly charge, pause. Ask: *Is this still serving me, or just charging me?*

Tools to Reclaim Control: Cut the Drift, Keep the Value

Tool: 2-Day Habit Reset – Uncover Your Subscription Drift

Objective: Quickly identify hidden or forgotten subscriptions and reset your relationship with recurring expenses.

Day 1: The Subscription Sweep

1. **Review All Accounts**

    - Open your bank and credit card statements from the last 60 days.

    - Scan for recurring charges, auto-renewals, or any transactions that repeat monthly, quarterly, or annually.

2. **List Them All Out**
   Create a simple table with the following columns:

    - **Service Name**

    - **Cost per Period**

    - **Frequency (Monthly/Annual)**

    - **Last Time You Used It**

    - **Would You Miss It? (Yes/No/Maybe)**

3. **Highlight Red Flags**
   Pay special attention to:

    - Services you haven't used in over a month.

- Subscriptions tied to past goals or versions of yourself (e.g., "January gym self," "wannabe chef self").

- Annual subscriptions that quietly renewed without notice.

Day 2: The Value Reality Check

1. **Sort Into Three Buckets**:

    - ✅ **Keep** – High use, high value, aligned with your current life.

    - ❌ **Cancel** – Rare or no use, emotionally or financially draining.

    - 🔄 **Reevaluate Later** – Uncertain value; set a calendar reminder to reassess in 30 days.

2. **Take Action Today**

    - Cancel at least *one* subscription that no longer serves you.

    - Set trial expiration reminders on your phone/calendar.

    - Switch any "Maybe" subscriptions to a lower tier or pause them if possible.

3. **Reflect**

Ask: *"What do I truly gain from each service, and what does it cost me in attention, identity, or money?"*

4. **Tool: 7-Day Subscription Use Tracker**

Objective: Build awareness of how often, and meaningfully, you use your current subscriptions. This tool helps differentiate *perceived* value from *actual* utility.

Day	Service Used	Time Spent	Value Felt (1–5)	Would I Miss It?
Mon				
Tue				
Wed				
Thu				
Fri				
Sat				
Sun				

How to Use This Tool:

- At the end of each day, jot down which subscription-based services you actually used.
- Rate the **value you received** from each use (1 = barely noticed, 5 = extremely useful or enjoyable).
- Consider whether you'd actually miss the service if it were gone.

End-of-Week Reflection Questions:

- Which subscriptions offered real value?
- Which ones did you never touch—but still pay for?
- What can you eliminate, downgrade, or replace with a one-time alternative?

Chapter 3: Emotional Spending Exposed

It's 11:47 p.m. You've had a brutal day, emails piling up, tension simmering from a passive-aggressive meeting, and dinner was cold leftovers eaten standing up. Now you're curled up on the couch, scrolling through your phone. Then, almost without thinking, you tap "Buy Now" on a pair of sneakers you don't need. Not because you've been eyeing them for weeks. Not because they're on sale. Just... because.

Sound familiar?

Or maybe it's the opposite: a rush of pride after a promotion leads you to book a luxury weekend getaway? On credit. A beautiful reward, until the bill arrives and the dopamine fades. Or maybe you've given a too-expensive gift to a friend you let down, trying to fix an emotional debt with financial currency.

We've all done it. Spent money not because we needed something, but because we *felt* something.

This is emotional spending in its most everyday form: subtle, sneaky, and deeply human.

What *Is* Emotional Spending?

Emotional spending happens when your wallet reacts to your feelings more than your needs. It's when you spend not because you've planned it, but because you're tired, stressed, lonely, bored, or, just as often, because you're happy, excited, or celebrating something.

Importantly, emotional spending isn't inherently "bad." After all, money is a tool, and sometimes, that spontaneous dinner out or thoughtful splurge can bring real joy. The problem arises when emotions drive spending unconsciously, when our financial choices become emotional reflexes rather than intentional decisions.

Because when that happens, it's easy to lose sight of what we actually value, and end up with a pile of packages, a drained bank account, and a nagging sense of regret.

Why Emotional Spending Deserves Your Attention ?

Understanding emotional spending isn't just about budgeting better. It's about uncovering the *invisible triggers* that hijack your decision-making, often without you realizing it.

Emotions are fast, powerful, and persuasive. They can completely override logic in the heat of the moment. That's why even the most financially savvy person can fall into a spending spiral after a tough day or during a holiday high. Whether it's a reward, a distraction, or a quick mood boost, spending can temporarily numb discomfort or amplify pleasure.

But here's the catch: those emotional highs fade fast. And the financial consequences tend to linger.

In a world where advertisers are skilled at tapping into your emotions, and stress is as common as coffee, emotional spending isn't just a quirk. It's a pattern. And it can quietly sabotage even the best financial intentions.

What You'll Learn in This Chapter ?

To help you spot, understand, and manage emotional spending, this chapter is broken down into three powerful subchapters:

1. Stress, Celebration, Guilt Spending
We'll explore the emotional "triggers" behind common spending behaviors, like revenge shopping after a bad breakup, retail therapy during stressful times, or overspending on loved ones out of guilt. You'll learn how different emotional states distort your perception of value and need.

2. HALT + B Framework
This practical tool, an extension of the classic HALT acronym (Hungry, Angry, Lonely, Tired) with *B* for *Bored*, will help you pause and identify emotional vulnerabilities before you hit "Add to Cart." Recognizing these emotional states in the moment is your first line of defense.

The Hidden Price of Emotional Spending

At its worst, emotional spending becomes a coping mechanism, a go-to way of dealing with life's ups and downs. It creates a feedback loop: emotional discomfort triggers spending, which may bring momentary relief, but often leads to regret, shame, or financial stress... which then triggers more emotional discomfort.

And so the cycle continues.

This pattern can silently erode your savings, inflate your debt, and undermine your financial confidence. But more than that, it can distance you from your deeper financial goals, freedom, security, choice, and the life you truly want to build.

Let's Pull Back the Curtain

So, here's the question:
What if you could learn to recognize the emotional triggers behind your spending, and take back control before emotions take over?

This chapter will help you do exactly that.

By the end, you won't just be more aware of how emotions shape your financial behavior, you'll be equipped with the tools to shift those habits. Not by denying yourself joy, but by aligning your spending with intention, self-awareness, and what actually matters to you.

Let's expose emotional spending for what it is, and reclaim your power over it.

3.1: Stress, Celebration, Guilt Spending

It's 8:00 p.m. on a Tuesday. You've had a grueling day, meetings ran long, your inbox exploded, and dinner is an afterthought. You're drained. So you order takeout, something indulgent, overpriced, and comforting. "I've earned this," you tell yourself, almost unconsciously, as you tap the "Place Order" button.

We've all been there. Sometimes we spend not because we need something, but because we're trying to feel something, relief, joy, control, connection. These are the moments when our emotions take the wheel. And often, we don't even realize they're driving.

This is emotional spending.

Emotional spending isn't about being reckless or irresponsible. It's about being human. Emotions, especially the intense ones, can nudge, or shove, us toward financial decisions we might not make with a clear head. And while not all emotional spending is harmful, when it becomes unconscious and habitual, it can lead to financial regret, confusion, or even deeper emotional strain.

In this subchapter, we'll explore three of the most common emotional triggers that influence spending behavior: **stress**, **celebration**, and **guilt**. Understanding these drivers is the first step toward building more conscious, values-aligned spending habits.

The Pull of Stress Spending

Stress spending is what happens when you try to buy your way out of discomfort. It's the late-night shopping spree after a bad day, the upgraded seat on your flight because you're feeling overwhelmed, or the spontaneous trip to the spa when everything feels like too much.

Stress activates our body's fight-or-flight system. Cortisol, the primary stress hormone, ramps up? And with it, our craving for quick comfort. Our brains, desperate for relief, push us toward short-term gratification. That could mean chocolate cake, an online shopping cart, or anything that offers the illusion of control or reward.

A 2022 study in *Psychology & Marketing* found that individuals experiencing elevated stress levels were more prone to make impulsive purchases? Particularly ones offering emotional comfort. In the moment, buying something can feel like reclaiming a sense of agency. But that temporary high fades, and often we're left with financial guilt layered on top of the original stress.

The problem with stress spending isn't the spending itself? it's the lack of intention behind it. When our wallets become coping tools, we start building a habit loop that ties emotional relief to financial behavior.

The Lure of Celebration Spending

Now, let's talk about the opposite end of the emotional spectrum: joy, success, pride. Positive emotions also trigger spending, but in a different costume. This is what we call celebration spending.

You land a new job, so you buy yourself a watch. Your friend gets engaged, so you book an expensive getaway to celebrate. Your child finishes the school year, so you take them on a surprise shopping trip. These moments feel good. And we want to mark them with something tangible, memorable, even Instagram-worthy.

Dopamine, the brain's "reward" chemical, spikes not only when we succeed, but also when we anticipate pleasure. Shopping, particularly when linked with celebration, hits that dopamine circuit hard. Add in social pressure, our culture's tendency to equate milestones with material rewards, and it's easy to see how celebration spending can spiral.

There's nothing wrong with treating yourself. In fact, planned rewards can enhance motivation. But unexamined celebration spending can lead to lifestyle inflation, where every victory, no matter how small, becomes an excuse for indulgence. Over time, the bar for "deserving a treat" gets lower, while the financial consequences stack higher.

The Weight of Guilt Spending

Of all emotional spending triggers, guilt may be the most invisible, and the most manipulative.

Guilt spending happens when we try to buy forgiveness, approval, or redemption. A parent who misses their child's recital overcompensates with an expensive toy. A partner who forgets an anniversary splurges on jewelry. A friend who feels distant sends an over-the-top gift.

At its core, guilt spending is an attempt to repair emotional damage with a material offering. It stems from a very human place, wanting to make things right. But often, it sidesteps the deeper work of addressing the source of guilt. Instead of apologizing, we give. Instead of reconnecting, we purchase.

This is especially common among overworked professionals and parents who feel torn between obligations. The narrative becomes: "If I can't give my time, I'll give something else, something expensive, to prove I care."

But here's the catch: most people don't want your money. They want your presence, your honesty, your attention. Guilt spending may temporarily soothe your discomfort, but it rarely resolves the emotional disconnect, and it can quietly erode your financial well-being.

The Common Thread: Emotional Loops

Whether driven by stress, celebration, or guilt, emotional spending follows a predictable loop:

1. **Trigger**: An emotional state arises, overwhelm, joy, shame.

2. **Impulse**: A desire to soothe, reward, or compensate kicks in.

3. **Action**: You make a purchase, often impulsive or unplanned.

4. **Relief (Temporary)**: You feel better… for a while.

5. **Consequence**: Financial regret, increased stress, or an unresolved emotional need.

These loops can become deeply ingrained, especially if they go unnoticed. They train the brain to see spending as the fastest route to emotional relief, creating a cycle that repeats with every high and low.

Emotional Spending Triggers Breakdown

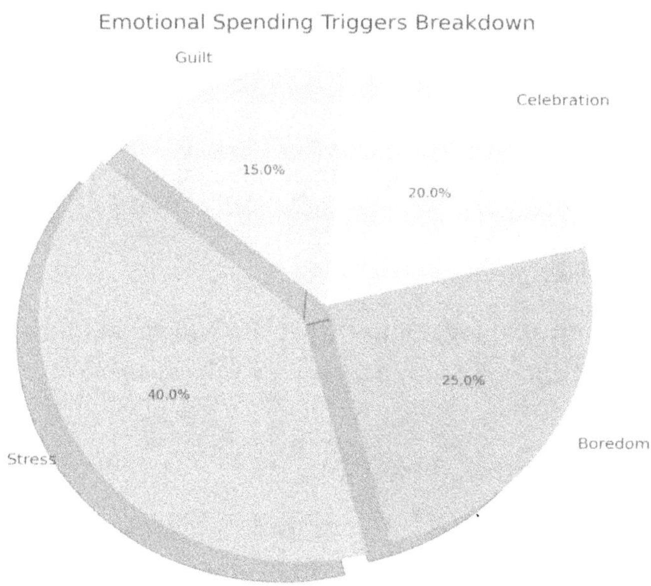

This visual illustrates the percentage breakdown of common emotional triggers that drive spending behavior. Based on general consumer behavior research, stress accounts for the largest share at 40%, followed by boredom (25%), celebration (20%), and guilt (15%).

It highlights the emotional complexity behind everyday financial decisions.

Reclaiming Control: Practical Tools

You don't need to eliminate emotional spending entirely, nor should you. Some purchases bring joy and meaning. The goal isn't restriction. It's awareness. Here's how to bring mindfulness to these spending habits:

1. Pause Before Purchasing

Create a 10-minute buffer between the impulse and the purchase. Ask yourself:

- What am I feeling right now?
- Is this a response to an emotion or a real need?
- Will this still feel worth it tomorrow?

This pause disrupts the loop and gives your rational mind a chance to re-enter the room.

2. Track Emotional Triggers

Use a spending journal to log not just what you bought, but how you felt when you bought it. Over time, patterns will emerge. You might notice:

- You shop more on stressful workdays.
- Celebrations trigger bigger-than-necessary purchases.
- Guilt leads you to overspend on others but not yourself.

Awareness is the first step to changing the pattern.

3. Set Boundaries, Not Bans

Give yourself permission to celebrate or decompress, but within limits. Create budgets for:

- Treats and rewards.
- Special occasions.
- Gifts and giving.

Boundaries prevent emotional spending from becoming financial sabotage.

4. Find Non-Financial Substitutes

Ask: "What emotional need am I trying to meet, and is there another way?"

- **Stress** → Try exercise, meditation, or simply unplugging.
- **Celebration** → Host a potluck, write a reflection, or plan a meaningful experience.
- **Guilt** → Offer a sincere apology, write a note, or spend quality time.

These alternatives can meet the same emotional need, without the financial hangover.

Closing Thought

Every spending decision tells a story. When driven by emotion, that story often reveals what we truly value, or what we're missing.

By understanding the emotional roots of stress, celebration, and guilt spending, you reclaim the power to respond intentionally, rather than react impulsively. You start to spend not just from habit, but from alignment, with your goals, your values, and your emotional truth.

The next time your finger hovers over the "Buy Now" button, ask yourself: *Is this for me, or for my feelings?* That question alone can change everything.

3.2: HALT + B Framework

Have you ever clicked "Add to Cart" not because you needed anything, but because you were just... off? Maybe it was after a draining day, or you were alone with your thoughts. Maybe you were irritated, or restless, or just plain hungry.

And suddenly, that $85 "self-care" kit or spontaneous DoorDash order made perfect sense.

Emotional spending often doesn't feel emotional in the moment. It feels like relief, reward, or escape. But when you look back, you realize the purchase wasn't really about the item, it was about your state of mind.

Enter the **HALT + B Framework**: a deceptively simple tool to help you catch yourself in these moments before they cost you.

What Is the HALT + B Framework?

HALT + B is an acronym that stands for:

- **Hungry**
- **Angry**
- **Lonely**

- **Tired**

- **Bored**

Originally adapted from addiction recovery practices, HALT was designed to help people pause and reflect before engaging in self-destructive behaviors. When you add **B** for *Bored*, the model becomes especially powerful for understanding consumer behavior.

The framework works like a psychological stop sign. When you feel an impulse to spend, especially on something unplanned, it prompts you to pause and ask: *Am I really making a financial decision… or am I just reacting to a feeling?*

Let's look at what each letter reveals.

The Triggers Behind the Letters

H – Hungry

Hunger isn't just physical—it's psychological. When your blood sugar is low, so is your impulse control. This doesn't just lead to buying overpriced snacks, it can also increase your likelihood of making poor, emotionally-driven decisions.

Ever notice how the "treat yourself" mindset hits hardest right before dinner? That's no coincidence. Hunger reduces cognitive control, making us more susceptible to quick dopamine hits… like clicking "Buy Now."

A – Angry

Anger creates a sense of powerlessness. Spending can become a form of regaining control, or venting. It's the retail version of a punch-the-wall moment.

You might justify it as a reward: *"They treated me like garbage at work today. I deserve this."* But underneath, it's a release valve.

L – Lonely

Loneliness is one of the most quietly powerful spending triggers. When we feel disconnected, we often look for comfort, belonging, or validation, sometimes through stuff.

That might be a new outfit to feel more confident, a gadget to fill the silence, or sending gifts to others just to feel remembered. But what we're really craving isn't the product, it's connection.

T – Tired

Fatigue doesn't just make you sleepy, it wears down your decision-making. A tired brain doesn't want to weigh long-term pros and cons. It wants quick wins and minimal friction.

That's why people often impulse-shop late at night, agree to recurring charges they'll later forget, or make financial decisions they wouldn't even consider with a clearer head.

B – Bored

Boredom is underestimated. A restless brain will seek stimulation anywhere, and online shopping is engineered to be both effortless and exciting.

Mindlessly scrolling, adding items to carts, browsing for fun… it's all an attempt to feel something. But in that dopamine-fueled haze, small purchases stack up fast.

Why HALT + B States Make Us Spend ?

From a psychological perspective, HALT + B states share a common theme: **depletion**.

When you're emotionally or physically depleted, your brain's prefrontal cortex, the part responsible for logic and long-term planning, goes offline. In its place, the limbic system takes over. That's the brain's reward center. It wants quick hits, not prudent choices.

Shopping offers exactly that. It provides a false sense of control, pleasure, and distraction, often within seconds. And the modern shopping experience, built for convenience and emotional appeal, only amplifies this vulnerability.

Behavioral science confirms it: people under emotional stress or low self-control are more likely to engage in **immediate-reward behaviors**, including spending.

Real-World Examples of HALT + B in Action

- **Hungry**: You're at the store after skipping lunch and suddenly find yourself loading up on gourmet snacks and energy drinks you'd usually pass by.

- **Angry**: After a tense argument, you order an expensive tech gadget to feel empowered or distracted.

- **Lonely**: You browse late-night shopping apps, rationalizing a new outfit or gift as a mood booster, when it's really about feeling seen.

- **Tired**: Too exhausted to cook, you subscribe to a premium meal plan you won't use, or buy a self-help course you'll never watch.

- **Bored**: You fill your Amazon cart during a work break just to kill time, not realizing you've spent $120 before lunch.

How to Use the HALT + B Framework ?

Here's how you can integrate HALT + B into your daily money habits:

1. Pause Before You Purchase

The moment an urge to spend strikes, hit the brakes, even for 60 seconds. Ask:

"Am I HALT + B right now?"

This creates a buffer between impulse and action.

2. Check In with Yourself

Run through each letter in your head. It's quick:

- Am I **hungry**?
- Am I **angry** about something?
- Do I feel **lonely** or disconnected?
- Am I **tired** or mentally foggy?
- Am I just **bored**?

Naming your state gives you power over it.

3. Address the Root, Not the Symptom

Don't shop over your feelings. Meet your actual need.

- Hungry? Eat first.
- Angry? Journal, breathe, or take a walk.
- Lonely? Call or text someone you trust.
- Tired? Nap, unplug, or rest.

- Bored? Move, create, or explore something non-commercial.

4. Track Patterns

Use a journal or notes app to log when HALT + B leads to spending impulses. You'll likely notice patterns, like always overspending on Friday nights or during long work meetings.

The Payoff of HALT + B Awareness

When you make HALT + B a habit, you:

- Spend less impulsively.
- Gain better insight into your emotional life.
- Learn to meet your needs without relying on consumption.
- Align your money decisions with your long-term values, not your short-term moods.

HALT + B Flowchart: Interrupt the Impulse

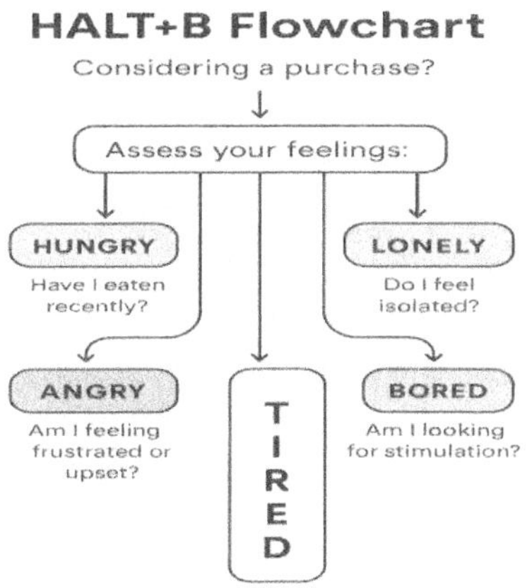

This visual flowchart offers a quick-reference decision tool that readers can use when they feel the urge to spend impulsively. By guiding them through a series of simple yes/no questions tied to emotional and physical states, Hungry, Angry, Lonely, Tired, or Bored, it helps interrupt the automatic spending loop and redirect attention to the root emotional trigger.

The flowchart acts as a behavioral pause button: a visual STOP sign before hitting "Buy Now."

One-Page HALT + B Self-Check Tool

You can print, bookmark, or write this out in your journal.

HALT + B Checklist: Emotional Spending Self-Check

Before You Spend, Ask:

✅ Am I **Hungry**?
→ Eat a nourishing snack or meal before deciding.

✅ Am I **Angry**?
→ Name the frustration. Walk, breathe, vent, don't shop to soothe.

✅ Am I **Lonely**?
→ Reach out. Send a message. Engage socially, without spending.

✅ Am I **Tired**?
→ Rest or recharge. Don't let fatigue make decisions.

✅ Am I **Bored**?
→ Find non-monetary stimulation: move, read, create, explore.

If you check ANY box, pause.
Delay the purchase. Return later, with a clear head.

Closing Thoughts

Money decisions aren't made in a vacuum. They're shaped by how you feel, what you need, and whether you're even aware of those needs in the moment.

The HALT + B Framework doesn't eliminate emotional spending, it makes it conscious. It puts you back in the driver's seat, allowing you to spend with intention rather than impulse.

So the next time a purchase calls your name, ask yourself:

Am I really shopping… or am I just HALT + B?

That single moment of mindfulness could save you money, and reveal what your emotions are truly asking for.

Part 2: Breaking the Spell

You've made it through the looking glass.

In *Part 1: The Mind Under the Money*, we uncovered the invisible strings, emotional triggers, subconscious needs, and psychological blind spots, that silently tug at your wallet. You learned that many spending choices aren't really choices at all, they're reactions. A dopamine hit here, a stress response there. Your brain, hardwired for comfort and certainty, often steers you toward financial behaviors that feel good in the moment but sabotage your long-term goals.

But here's the good news: awareness is power.
And now, it's time to use that power to *break the spell.*

Imagine walking through a theme park built entirely to separate you from your money. Everything is engineered to keep you entertained, distracted, and spending, from the music in the background to the smell of freshly baked cookies pumped into the air. That's not fantasy. It's how modern marketing works.

In the first chapter of this section, **Impulse Buying Is Engineered**, we'll peel back the curtain on the psychology of consumer design. You'll discover how brands use your biology against you, leveraging scarcity, urgency, and emotion to make sure your logical brain never gets a chance to weigh in. From the color of a "Buy Now" button to the countdown clock in your cart, you'll see how meticulously your impulses are being nudged, poked, and prodded.

But it's not just the world outside you.
It's your own mind, too.

In the second chapter, **Brain Biases That Bankrupt You**, we'll step inside the cognitive trapdoors that even the smartest spenders fall into. Why do you hold onto a subscription you never use? (Hello, sunk cost fallacy.) Why does losing $50 hurt more than gaining $50 feels good? (That's loss aversion.) Why are you sure *this* time your big purchase will finally make you happy? (Meet the optimism bias.) These mental shortcuts were meant to help us survive, but in today's economy, they can quietly drain our bank accounts.

Here's the truth:
You are not broken.
You are not weak.
You are human, and your brain is doing exactly what it was designed to do.

But what was once useful in the wild isn't always wise in a shopping cart.

Part 2 is where you begin to outsmart your own instincts. By understanding the design of the consumer world *and* the design of your brain, you'll be equipped to slow down, step back, and make money decisions with clarity, not compulsion.

This is where awareness turns into agency.
This is where the spell starts to lift.

Are you ready to see what's really happening behind the screen, the shelf, and the swipe?
Let's pull back the curtain, and take your power back.

Chapter 4: Impulse Buying Is Engineered

You didn't plan to buy the extra scented candle.
Or the limited-edition hoodie.
Or the wireless earbuds that just *happened* to be 20% off today.

And yet, there they are on your receipt. Again.

If this sounds familiar, you're not alone. Studies show that **over 60% of purchases are impulse buys**. And here's the kicker: this isn't because you're bad with money or lacking willpower. It's because you're shopping in environments *specifically designed* to make you act on impulse.

Impulse buying isn't an accident. It's architecture.

From the moment you step into a store, or open an app, you're entering a carefully choreographed experience. Every scent, sound, color, layout, notification, and "Only 3 left!" message is part of a psychological blueprint engineered to bypass your better judgment. Retailers aren't just selling products, they're selling *moments of surrender*. And they've spent billions studying how to trigger them.

In this chapter, we'll explore the machinery behind this emotional manipulation.

In **Store Psychology, Digital Traps**, you'll learn how your environment silently shapes your spending. Ever wonder why fresh flowers and bakery scents greet you at the grocery store entrance? Why your favorite online store always recommends "customers also bought…" just as you're about to check out? These aren't happy accidents, they're subtle psychological nudges designed to shift your attention from logic to emotion.

Then, in **tools: Anti-Cart Strategy, No Impulse Week**, we shift from awareness to action. You'll discover practical ways to disarm these marketing tactics before they reach your wallet. Whether it's building a mental "impulse firewall," rethinking your digital shopping habits, or committing to a no-spend challenge, you'll gain tools that give you back control, without giving up joy or convenience.

Here's the truth most brands won't tell you:
Impulse buying isn't a reflection of your discipline, it's a reflection of *their design.*

But design can be hacked.
And behavior can be rewired.

This chapter is your wake-up call, and your shield. Once you understand how the trap is set, you stop being the prey and start becoming the architect of your own financial decisions.

So if you've ever looked at your bank statement and thought, *How did I spend so much without meaning to?*, you're in the right place.

Let's step behind the curtain and see how the spell is cast, so you can finally break free.

4.1: Store Psychology, Digital Traps

Ever walked into a store for one thing, let's say toothpaste, and walked out with $67 worth of snacks, candles, and novelty socks you hadn't even thought about five minutes prior? That's not a failure of willpower. That's design.

Impulse buying is not a fluke. It's not about personal weakness or momentary lapse. It's a carefully engineered outcome. Retailers, both physical and digital, meticulously craft environments that nudge, seduce, and subtly push you into spending more than you planned. And they do it by targeting the very psychology that governs your decisions, usually without you even noticing.

This chapter pulls back the curtain on how your spending decisions are shaped long before you reach for your wallet or click "Buy Now."

The Architecture of Impulse: How Stores Shape Your Spending

When you enter a supermarket, you're not just walking into a store, you're entering a behavioral laboratory. Everything, from the smell in the air to the position of the shopping carts, is optimized to encourage you to buy more.

Strategic Store Layouts

Essential items like milk, eggs, or bread are rarely near the entrance. Instead, they're placed at the very back, forcing you to walk past aisles packed with products you didn't come for but might suddenly want. This isn't random. It's a deliberate detour designed to expose you to as many impulse triggers as possible.

Sensory Cues

Stores don't just sell products, they sell experiences. Research shows that warm lighting, pleasant scents (like freshly baked cookies or vanilla), and curated music can elevate mood and reduce decision fatigue, making you more likely to linger and spend. For example, Abercrombie & Fitch was notorious for dim lighting, pulsing music, and strong cologne, all creating an immersive environment that bypassed logic and played directly to emotion.

Product Placement

Eye-level is buy-level. The most profitable or enticing products are placed right where your eyes naturally land. Kid-targeted items like sugary cereals or toys? They're placed lower, right where little ones can see and reach. Sale tags, "new" labels, and bright colors are strategically used to grab your attention even when your shopping list is short.

And then there's the **checkout lane gauntlet**, a masterclass in last-minute temptation. Candy bars, lip balm, phone chargers, small, low-resistance items placed to capitalize on your final moment of distraction. The average person spends an extra $5 to $10 while waiting to pay.

These tactics work because they create what psychologists call a "hot state", a condition where your emotional brain (the limbic system) takes over and urges you to seek instant gratification.

How Stores and Screens Trigger Impulse Spending

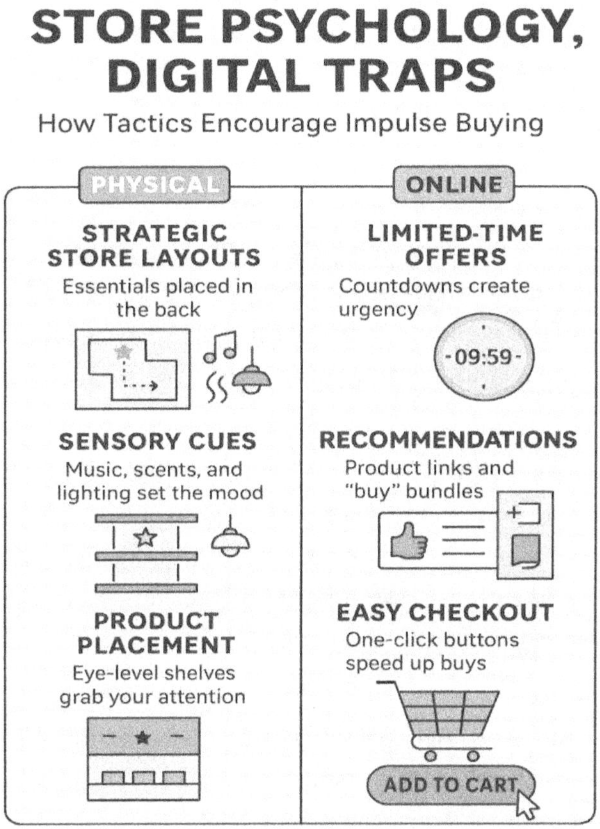

This visual breakdown reveals the core tactics used by physical stores and digital platforms to encourage unplanned spending. From strategic layouts and sensory cues to personalized algorithms and scarcity triggers, each layer is designed to bypass rational decision-making and activate your emotional brain.

Digital Traps: Impulse Buying in the Age of Algorithms

If physical stores are behavioral labs, online platforms are full-blown psychological war zones.

With no aisles to walk and no checkout lines to navigate, e-commerce has supercharged impulse buying by removing nearly every friction point, and replacing it with tailored nudges. Amazon doesn't just show you what you came for, it shows you what you *might* want, what others bought, what's trending, and what's running out fast.

Scarcity and Urgency

You've likely seen it: "Only 3 left in stock!" or "Deal ends in 2 hours!" These aren't always real-time inventory metrics, they're behavioral triggers. The mere suggestion of scarcity triggers fear of missing out, overriding your logical evaluation of whether you *need* the item.

Bundling and Cross-Selling

The "Frequently Bought Together" section is a perfect example of psychological suggestion. If you're buying a laptop, suddenly a mouse, keyboard, and carrying case appear, and feel almost necessary. It's the digital version of a friend whispering, "You may as well…"

Effortless Checkout

One-click buying and saved payment info eliminate hesitation. You never have to pull out your card or even second-guess. The goal is to compress decision time and stretch spending.

Personalization Algorithms

Online stores know what you browse, how long you linger, what colors you prefer, and when you're most likely to click. This isn't just convenience, it's behavioral manipulation disguised as customization.

Social Commerce

Instagram, TikTok, and Pinterest aren't just social media, they're marketplaces. When influencers showcase products "you didn't know you needed," it feels casual, but it's designed to exploit trust and emotional contagion. Aesthetic, aspirational content turns product placement into personal aspiration.

Why These Tactics Work: The Psychology Beneath the Surface

These marketing strategies work because they hijack hardwired psychological principles:

- **Scarcity Bias**: We place higher value on things that seem rare or limited, even when we don't need them.

- **Loss Aversion**: We fear losing out more than we desire gaining something. That's why "ending soon" deals are so effective, they tap into the emotional cost of missing out.

- **Social Proof**: When we see an item labeled "Best Seller" or "Trending," we assume its popularity signals quality, which nudges us toward the purchase.

- **Cognitive Ease**: The smoother the shopping experience, the more likely we are to keep going. One-click buying, seamless browsing, and auto-saved data all reduce resistance, allowing emotion to lead the charge.

Each of these principles bypasses your rational, long-term thinking in favor of short-term reward, and they stack on top of each other to create an irresistible buying momentum.

The Cumulative Toll: Micro-Spending, Macro-Consequences

The damage to impulse buying isn't just in the big-ticket items, it's in the small, repeated, emotionally-driven purchases that accumulate quietly over time.

A $14 face mask here, a $27 candle there, a $9 express shipping fee "just this once", these micro-decisions may feel trivial in isolation, but they add up. Research shows that up to **50% of all consumer purchases are unplanned**, and the average person spends over **$5,400 a year on impulse buys**.

More troubling is the emotional aftermath. Impulse purchases often lead to regret, clutter, or even guilt, particularly if the item goes unused or contributes to financial stress. The shopping temporarily numbs a feeling (boredom, stress, loneliness), but it doesn't solve it. And that unresolved emotion can lead to yet another impulse buy.

Awareness as Armor

The good news? Once you see the blueprint, you can stop being a pawn on the board.

Understanding that impulse buying is engineered helps shift the narrative. It's not you being "bad with money"—it's that you're navigating systems designed to disarm your self-control. But once you recognize these traps, you're no longer walking blind.

In the next subchapter, you'll learn tactical defenses: how to pause, rethink, and regain your financial agency using tools like the **Anti-Cart Strategy** and **No Impulse Week**. These aren't about denial or strict budgeting, they're about conscious, empowered spending.

Because the strongest antidote to manipulation… is awareness.

4.2 : TOOLS: Anti-Cart Strategy, No Impulse Week

TOOL #1: The Anti-Cart Strategy

Break the trance. Question the cart. Spend with intention.

Impulse buying thrives on speed, ease, and emotion. The **Anti-Cart Strategy** interrupts that flow. It works whether you're in a store aisle or scrolling through your phone at midnight. The goal is to inject **intentionality** into the decision-making process before money leaves your account.

How It Works:

Whenever you're about to make a non-essential purchase (online or in-store), pause and ask yourself these five questions:

1. **Did I plan to buy this before I saw it?**
   If it wasn't already on your list, it's likely an emotional decision, not a rational one.

2. **What feeling am I trying to satisfy?**
   Are you bored, anxious, lonely, or stressed? Recognizing the emotional trigger helps break the cycle.

3. **Can I wait 24 hours?**
   Set a "cooling off" period. Most impulses fade once the emotional urgency passes.

4. **Do I already own something similar?**
   Impulse buys often duplicate what we already have—highlighting a want, not a need.

5. **What will this cost me long-term?**
   Not just in dollars, but in space, clutter, attention, and potential regret.

Pro Tip: Create a "Wish List" folder or note on your phone. Instead of clicking "Buy Now," add the item to the list. If you still want it in a week, revisit—but odds are, the impulse will be gone.

Why It Works:

The Anti-Cart Strategy shifts you from a **reactive** to a **reflective** mindset. By slowing down the process, it gives your rational brain (the prefrontal cortex) a chance to override the emotional brain (limbic system), which retailers rely on to drive fast decisions.

It doesn't mean never buying things you enjoy, it means **buying with awareness instead of impulse**.

TOOL #2: No Impulse Week

Hit pause. Reset your habits. Reclaim control.

No Impulse Week is a behavioral detox. It's a simple but powerful challenge: for seven days, you commit to **buying only what's essential**, and deliberately avoid all non-essential purchases.

The Rules:

1. **Essentials Only.**
   Groceries, bills, prescriptions-yes. Everything else-no. No clothes, no gadgets, no scented candles, no $9 lattes "just because."

2. **Track Every Urge.**
   Keep a running list of everything you *wanted* to buy. Include what triggered the impulse (Instagram ad, boredom, stress, etc.).

3. **Note the Emotion.**
   With each urge, write down how you felt in that moment. You'll start to see patterns, emotional states that push you toward spending.

4. **Reflect on Day 7.**
   Review your list. How many things do you still want? How many were purely emotional spikes? How did it feel to say no?

Optional Accountability Boost: Tell a friend or partner you're doing the challenge. Social support strengthens follow-through.

Why It Works:

No Impulse Week isn't about deprivation, it's about **recalibrating your buying reflex**. Most of us spend automatically, driven by emotion and engineered environments. This exercise brings those habits into the light.

By delaying gratification and observing your impulses without judgment, you build **financial self-awareness**, and that's the foundation of long-term control.

Summary Checklist :

🛒 ANTI-CART STRATEGY	📅 NO IMPULSE WEEK
? Did I plan this?	✅ Buy essentials only
😟 What am I feeling?	📝 Track each urge
☐ Can I wait 24 hours?	😊 Note the emotion
🎁 Do I own something similar?	🔍 Reflect after 7 days
💸 What's the long-term cost?	👥 Share for support

Closing Words:

These tools are not about guilt. They're about **reclaiming the driver's seat**.

Every time you use the Anti-Cart Strategy or complete a No Impulse Week, you're strengthening your financial decision-making muscles. The more conscious you become, the less power these invisible triggers will have over your money, and your peace of mind.

Chapter 5: Brain Biases That Bankrupt You

Why do we keep paying for gym memberships we never use? Why do we convince ourselves that a $400 concert ticket is worth it, because "we already spent the money", even if we're too exhausted to go? And why does it feel like everyone else is making smarter money moves than we are… even when we're drowning in Amazon boxes we don't remember ordering?

These moments aren't flukes. They're not lapses in judgment or signs you're "bad with money." They're the product of your brain doing exactly what it was designed to do: take shortcuts.

These shortcuts, known as **cognitive biases**, help us make fast decisions in a complex world. But when it comes to money, they often lead us down the wrong path, toward **overspending**, **financial stress**, and **costly regret**.

Your Brain's Hidden Spending Traps

Imagine your brain as an autopilot system. Most of the time, that autopilot does a pretty good job. It helps you decide what to wear, how to respond in conversations, even what to eat for lunch, without paralyzing overthinking. But in high stakes decisions like spending, saving, and investing, that same system can backfire.

Take **FOMO**, the fear of missing out. It's not just a social media buzzword. It's a powerful emotional driver that makes you say "yes" to things your bank account says "no" to. A limited-time sale, a hot stock tip, a vacation everyone else seems to be taking, FOMO makes you believe you're losing something by not spending.

Or the **sunk cost fallacy**: when you keep throwing money (or time) at something because you've already invested so much in it. Like the gym membership you never use… but won't cancel. Or the overpriced purse you keep justifying because "it was expensive."

Then there's **optimism bias**, our brain's tendency to believe things will work out fine, even when the data suggests otherwise. It's why we underestimate future expenses, overestimate our future income, and believe we'll "catch up on savings later." Spoiler: later often never comes.

These aren't just quirks. They're **predictable patterns** baked into how the human brain works. And left unchecked, they're the silent saboteurs of your financial goals.

What This Chapter Will Help You Uncover ?

In this chapter, we're going deep into the psychology of spending, into the brain's blind spots that silently steer your financial choices. You'll learn:

- How **FOMO** exploits your fear of exclusion and how marketers weaponize it to get you to spend now and think later.

- Why the **sunk cost fallacy** keeps you stuck in bad purchases, failing investments, or lifestyle choices that no longer serve you.

- How **optimism bias** creates unrealistic expectations that derail your budgeting, saving, and long-term planning.

These biases aren't flaws. They're part of how we're wired. But once you see them, you can *disarm* them. You can pause. Reframe. Choose differently.

Tools to Rewire Your Thinking

To help you put this insight into action, you'll get hands-on tools designed to challenge the biases that bankrupt your decision-making:

- The **Bias Buster Cards**: Quick mental prompts you can use in real-time to challenge distorted thinking before it leads to a costly choice.

- The **Wallet Drainer Quiz**: A revealing self-assessment that helps you identify which biases are draining your wallet the fastest, and what to do about them.

These aren't just tips. They're cognitive tools that help you think like a behavioral psychologist… when your money's on the line.

Awareness Is the First Step to Freedom

Cognitive biases are sneaky. They don't announce themselves. They whisper. They nudge. They justify. And they're so good at it that most people don't even know they're being influenced.

But that's about to change.

By the end of this chapter, you'll have a clear lens on the invisible scripts running in the background of your financial life. You'll see the traps *before* you fall into them. And better yet, you'll know how to climb out when you do.

Ready to outsmart the brain tricks that sabotage your wallet? Let's dive in, and start rewriting the mental scripts that shape your spending story.

5.1: FOMO, Sunk Cost, Optimism Bias

Why do we spend money on things we don't need, or hold onto bad investments long after they've stopped serving us? The answer isn't always about logic, it's about brain traps. Subtle, invisible distortions in how we think about money. They creep in, masked as gut feelings, but what they truly are, are cognitive biases.

Cognitive biases are mental shortcuts. They evolved to help our brains make quick decisions without getting overwhelmed by every piece of information. In the wild, that worked beautifully, deciding instantly whether to flee from a rustling bush might have meant the difference between life and death. But in modern life, these shortcuts often misfire, especially around complex, emotional domains like money.

This subchapter explores three of the most influential, and financially dangerous, biases: **FOMO (Fear of Missing Out), the Sunk Cost Fallacy, and Optimism Bias**. Each one is a stealthy saboteur of smart money decisions. Let's pull them into the light.

FOMO: Fear of Missing Out

FOMO whispers, "Everyone else is doing it, you'll regret not joining in." And that whisper gets louder every time we scroll through curated Instagram vacations, TikTok shopping hauls, or flash sale countdowns.

FOMO is rooted in **social comparison** and the scarcity mindset. Evolutionarily, being part of the group meant survival. Missing out might have meant being excluded from shared resources or protection. Today, that instinct hasn't left us, it's just been redirected to discount codes and destination weddings.

We see a limited-time offer and think, "If I don't buy this now, I'll miss my chance." A friend posts about their $400 concert experience, and suddenly we feel like our weekend is incomplete. We weren't even planning to go, but now we can't stop thinking about it.

Social media amplifies FOMO like a megaphone. Algorithms push the most aspirational content to the top, vacations, gadgets, experiences, most of which come with a price tag. When we see it, we don't just want the product; we crave the **feeling** of being included, of keeping up, of not missing out on life.

Financially, FOMO leads to:

- Impulse purchases
- Debt accumulation
- Abandoned financial goals

What's worse: it often disguises itself as self-care or spontaneity. But in reality, it's emotional spending disguised as connection.

The Sunk Cost Fallacy

Imagine you've paid $120 for a concert, but come show day, you're sick, tired, and the weather's awful. You go anyway, even though you won't enjoy it. Why? "Because I already paid for it."

That's the sunk cost fallacy in action.

A **sunk cost** is money you've already spent and can't recover. Rationally, past costs shouldn't affect future decisions. But emotionally, we cling to what we've paid, whether it's money, time, or effort, and that attachment makes us double down on bad choices.

Real-life examples:

- Staying subscribed to a premium streaming service you rarely use, because "you've already paid through the year."
- Refusing to sell a failing investment because you don't want to "lock in the loss."
- Pouring more money into a business that's bleeding cash because you've "put too much into it to stop now."

Psychologically, the sunk cost fallacy is driven by:

- **Loss aversion**: We hate losing more than we like winning.
- **Self-justification**: We want to believe our past decisions were right.
- **Identity protection**: Quitting feels like failure, and failure feels personal.

The consequence? We throw good money after bad, delay better options, and keep ourselves stuck, financially and emotionally.

Optimism Bias

Optimism bias is the internal narrator that says, "It'll all work out," even when the facts say otherwise. It's why people go over budget, ignore warnings, or jump into financial commitments without a backup plan.

At its core, optimism bias is a **belief that negative outcomes are less likely to happen to us** than to other people. It's why we think we'll pay off that credit card before the interest hits, even though we never have before. Or why we assume our side hustle will grow fast enough to cover next month's rent.

Examples include:

- Underestimating how much a home renovation will actually cost
- Assuming you'll start saving "soon" even with no concrete plan

- Believing your income will rise fast enough to justify a big purchase

This bias is partially driven by **wishful thinking** and an avoidance of discomfort. It feels good to believe everything will be fine. It feels bad to consider the worst-case scenario. But ignoring those risks can mean walking into financial disaster without a parachute.

Optimism bias doesn't just affect spending, it warps our ability to plan, save, and insure against future uncertainty. The cost isn't just monetary, it's stress, burnout, and the feeling of always playing catch-up.

Recognizing the Patterns: Your Brain on Bias

All three of these biases, FOMO, sunk cost, and optimism bias, have one thing in common: **they bypass rational thinking**. They exploit emotion, fear, hope, and identity. They don't feel like biases; they feel like gut instincts or "common sense."

That's what makes them so dangerous.

These biases are silent decision-makers. They influence:

- What you buy
- What you keep
- What you hope for

They distort how you evaluate risk, value, and priorities, without you realizing it. Over time, they drain your wallet, clutter your life, and shake your financial confidence.

Breaking the Bias Loop

The good news? Once you can name a bias, you can challenge it. Awareness gives you leverage.

In the next section, you'll find tools to do exactly that, starting with the **Bias Buster Cards**, quick-reference prompts designed to help you interrupt flawed thinking in real time. You'll also take the **Wallet Drainer Quiz**, a short, sharp inventory to help you identify which biases most often sabotage your spending.

You don't need to eliminate these biases. Furthermore, you just need to recognize them when they appear. That awareness alone can change the trajectory of your financial life.

Because the real danger isn't the bias, it's believing your thoughts are always telling you the truth.

5.2: Tools - Bias Buster Cards & The Wallet Drainer Quiz

Cognitive biases don't announce themselves.
They slip in unnoticed, disguised as instinct, convenience, or optimism, quietly steering your financial decisions off course. But once you learn to spot them, you gain something rare in personal finance: **leverage over your own psychology**.

This subchapter introduces two practical tools designed to help you identify and interrupt those invisible biases in real time: **Bias Buster Cards** and **The Wallet Drainer Quiz**.

These aren't gimmicks. They're mental speed bumps, strategic pauses you insert when your brain is about to make an emotionally hijacked decision. Used regularly, these tools train you to pause, question, and choose, rather than react, rationalize, and regret.

Bias Buster Cards

Instant Interruptions for Irrational Decisions

Bias Buster Cards are concise, psychologically targeted prompts that break the autopilot of emotionally driven spending. Think of them as flashcards for your decision-making system. Each card targets a specific bias, like **FOMO**, **Sunk Cost Fallacy**, or **Optimism Bias**, and creates a moment of friction before a potentially regrettable financial choice.

How to Use Them ?

- Keep a printed set in your wallet, at your desk, or near your digital spending devices.

- Before any purchase above a personal threshold (e.g., $50), draw a card? Or mentally ask yourself its question.

- Use them during moments of urgency, emotional fatigue, or when you sense you're justifying a decision.

Sample Cards

□ **FOMO**

"Would I still want this if no one else knew I bought it?"

Exposes whether your motivation is internal or based on social comparison.

● **Sunk Cost Fallacy**

"If I weren't already invested, would I choose this again today?"

Reframes your decision as if you were starting from scratch, helping you let go of past financial inertia.

□ **Optimism Bias**

"What's the worst realistic outcome, and am I financially prepared for it?"

Doesn't kill your optimism, it disciplines it with preparedness.

○ **Universal Reframe**

"If I delay this decision for 24 hours, what might change?"

Most biases lose their power with time. Distance restores clarity.

Tip: Create your own cards based on personal patterns. The point isn't perfection, it's presence.

The Wallet Drainer Quiz

Identify the Bias Costing You the Most

Some cognitive biases work like background music, shaping your decisions quietly, constantly, and invisibly. The Wallet Drainer Quiz helps you bring them to the surface. This self-assessment reveals the dominant psychological pattern draining your finances and points you toward specific corrective strategies.

What This Quiz Does ?

- Identifies your primary financial bias: FOMO, Sunk Cost, or Optimism.
- Reveals your personal "risk zone" for impulsive or irrational spending.
- Recommends tailored Bias Buster Cards and mindset shifts.

Sample Quiz Statements

(Answer Yes or No)

1. *Do you often buy things on sale, even if you hadn't planned to?*
   → FOMO / Scarcity Bias

2. *Have you kept a subscription because "you already paid for it"?*
   → Sunk Cost Fallacy

3. *Do you assume your finances will improve, even without a clear plan?*
   → Optimism Bias

4. *Have you bought something to keep up with others on social media?*
   → FOMO + Social Proof

5. *Do you have unused items you once thought you'd use "someday"?*
   → Impulse + Sunk Cost

6. *Do you underestimate your monthly lifestyle costs?*
   → Optimism + Budget Blindness

7. *Have you made purchases to "motivate" a new version of yourself (e.g., gym gear, planners)?*
   → Optimism Bias meets Emotional Spending

Scoring Guide

- **0–2 Yeses:** Your decision-making is largely bias-resistant.

- **3–5 Yeses:** Biases are quietly influencing your choices. Build awareness now.

- **6–7 Yeses:** Biases are running the show. It's time for a strategic mental reset.

At the end of the quiz, you'll know which bias is draining your wallet the most, and what you can do to stop it.

Why These Tools Matter ?

You can't out-earn a bias.
You can't out-budget it either. If left unchecked, these psychological distortions will sabotage your savings, inflate your lifestyle, and quietly normalize financial stress.

But you can **interrupt** them.
You can **question** them.
And you can **slow the moment down**, just enough to make a conscious, values-based decision instead of a reflexive one.

Bias Buster Cards and **The Wallet Drainer Quiz** don't require perfection. They require **presence**. They give you a structure to stay mentally engaged in your money choices, and to build a habit of checking in with yourself, not just your bank balance.

Part 3: Rewiring for Wealth

Transforming Your Mind from Financial Saboteur to Financial Ally

What if your brain could become your greatest financial asset, not your biggest obstacle?

That's not a metaphor. It's neuroscience.

Your brain isn't hardwired for wealth, it's wired for survival, instant gratification, and short-term comfort. Left unchecked, that wiring pulls you toward impulse buys, lifestyle creep, and emotional spending. But here's the powerful truth: **your brain is not fixed.** It's a living, rewritable system. And that means the same brain that once sabotaged your savings can be trained to grow them.

You've already done the hard psychological excavation. In *Part 1*, you uncovered the invisible triggers, stress, boredom, guilt, social pressure, that silently shaped your spending. In *Part 2*, you began breaking the spell, learning how to interrupt those biases and regain control. Now, in *Part 3*, we turn the page to a new story, one where you're not just reacting less... but **rewiring more**.

This is where lasting change happens.

Rewiring for Wealth isn't about budgeting harder or feeling guilty less. It's about **training your brain** to make powerful money decisions automatically. Just as a musician builds muscle memory through scales, or an athlete refines instincts through repetition, you can reprogram your mental habits around money, **consciously, intentionally, and permanently**.

The lead chapter, *Rewiring the Brain for Wealth*, shows you how to do exactly that. You'll learn how to:

- **Replace self-defeating financial habits** with behaviors that build long-term security and growth.

- Use **proven neuroscience tools**, like habit stacking, visualization, and reframing, to recondition your brain's reward systems.

- Build **automated decision pathways** that align with your goals, so that saving, investing, and resisting temptation become second nature, not a struggle.

You don't need more willpower. You need better wiring. And that starts here.

So if you've ever felt like your brain is working *against* your financial goals, this is the part of the book that hands you the blueprint to flip the script. Financial freedom doesn't begin with your bank account. **It begins with your beliefs, your habits, and your neural pathways.**

This is your opportunity to become the architect of your financial future, not just reacting to money, but mastering it.

Ready to turn your brain into your greatest financial ally?
Let's rewire it, one thought, one habit, one wealthy decision at a time.

Chapter 6: Rewiring the Brain for Wealth

How to Train Your Mind to Think Like a Builder, Not a Bystander ?

What if you could rewire your brain to think like a wealth builder, not a spender?
Not with more willpower. Not with stricter budgets. But by literally reshaping the way your brain fires when you face financial decisions.

Neuroscience has a word for this: **neuroplasticity**, the brain's incredible ability to rewire itself based on repeated thought patterns and behaviors. And in this chapter, you're going to learn how to harness that power.

Up to this point in the book, you've taken a courageous journey. You've uncovered the hidden forces that drive your financial behavior. You've exposed the emotional triggers, the subconscious biases, and the spending habits that kept you stuck. Furthermore, you've broken the spell. **Now it's time to rebuild, on purpose.**

This chapter is your turning point.

We're no longer playing defense against impulsive spending or emotional traps. In *Rewiring the Brain for Wealth*, we go on offense. You'll learn how to create new mental habits, **abundance-oriented, intentional, and goal-aligned**, that shift you from reacting to your money to **mastering it**.

We start by exploring one of the most powerful mindset shifts in financial psychology: moving from a **scarcity mindset** ("there's never enough") to an **abundance mindset** ("there's more than enough when I focus and plan"). This isn't toxic positivity. It's a researched, practical approach to retraining your brain to look for opportunities instead of threats. You'll see how even subtle changes in your self-talk, perspective, and language can open the mental space for smarter decisions.

Next, we introduce the idea of **friction tactics**, small, intentional speed bumps that interrupt impulsive spending. These aren't barriers meant to frustrate you, they're strategic delays that give your rational brain time to catch up. Just as successful people automate saving, they also *intentionally slow down* their spending. You'll learn how to build these friction points into your everyday life, digitally and physically.

Then come the tools, your behavioral rewiring toolkit:

- The **30-Day Reset**, a practical, science-backed way to break entrenched habits and build new, wealth-supporting routines.

- The **Spending Strategy Map**, your personal blueprint for aligning your money with your values, so that each dollar serves a purpose, not a passing emotion.

Throughout this chapter, we'll ground these strategies in psychology and neuroscience. You'll learn how **habit loops** form in the brain, and how to disrupt and redesign them. You'll discover how **dopamine** drives spending urges and how to redirect that reward-seeking system toward long-term goals. And you'll build the emotional and cognitive scaffolding needed to make financial decisions from a place of clarity, not compulsion.

Most importantly, you'll prove to yourself that lasting change doesn't require a personality transplant. It requires a plan—and **practice**.

Rewiring your brain for wealth isn't about becoming someone else. It's about becoming **the version of you that money no longer controls**. The one who sees clearly, acts intentionally, and builds wealth with confidence.

So if you're ready to stop spinning in old financial cycles and start constructing a future with purpose, this chapter is your blueprint.

Let's rewire. Your brain, and your wealth, are ready.

6.1: Abundance Thinking, Friction Tactics

How Mindset and Micro-Barriers Can Rewire Your Spending Habits ?

Two people. Same income. Same bills. Same city. One feels constantly behind, anxious, and trapped in a cycle of "just getting by." The other feels calm, empowered, and confident about their future. What's the difference?
It's not luck. It's not privilege. It's not even income.

It's mindset, and how they manage their impulses.

One lives in scarcity. The other thinks in abundance.
One spends reactively. The other builds in friction.

This subchapter is about adopting these two powerful shifts, **abundance thinking** and **friction tactics**, to break free from old financial habits and start rewiring your brain for wealth.

Because the truth is, *it's not just what you earn, it's how you think and what you do in the moments that matter.*

The Power of Abundance Thinking

Abundance thinking is a mindset rooted in the belief that there's enough, enough opportunity, enough time, enough money, to meet your needs and build your future. It doesn't mean denying challenges or pretending everything is perfect. It means choosing to focus on what's possible instead of what's missing.

Scarcity thinking, by contrast, is driven by fear—*there's never enough.* It whispers, "Better spend this now, you may not get another chance." It nudges you toward impulse buying, hoarding, or avoiding long-term planning altogether because it all feels out of reach.

Behavioral science shows that scarcity doesn't just affect emotions, it **narrows our focus** and impairs decision-making. In a famous study, researchers found that people experiencing financial scarcity (even hypothetically) scored significantly lower on cognitive tests. Scarcity literally **shrinks your mental bandwidth**, making it harder to make wise, long-term financial choices.

Abundance thinking expands that bandwidth. It creates mental space to breathe, plan, and act with intention.

Take two people faced with an unexpected expense. A scarcity thinker may panic and swipe a credit card, worried this crisis proves they'll "never get ahead." An abundance thinker sees the same event as a temporary setback and asks What *can I learn from this? What's within my control?*

The shift sounds subtle. But it's the difference between spiraling into anxiety and taking calm, focused action.

And here's the best part: **abundance isn't a personality trait. It's a practice.** It's something you can train your brain to adopt.

Practical Steps to Cultivate Abundance Thinking

So how do you start thinking abundantly, especially if you've lived with money anxiety for years?

Here are four powerful practices:

1. **Practice Gratitude Daily**
   Write down three things you're grateful for related to money or resources. It could be as simple as "I had food today," "I paid my bills this month," or "I have the ability to learn about money." Gratitude activates neural circuits tied to optimism and long-term thinking.

2. **Reframe Financial Challenges**
   Instead of saying, *"I can't afford this,"* try, *"How can I afford this responsibly?"* This shifts your brain from resignation to resourcefulness. It engages your creative problem-solving

instead of triggering defeat.

3. **Visualize Financial Success**
   Picture your future self—five years from now—living with financial stability and freedom. What habits got you there? What did you stop doing? Visualization helps rewire the brain by reinforcing your identity as someone who builds wealth.

4. **Curate Your Environment**
   Follow creators, podcasts, and communities that promote intentional living and smart money habits. What you feed your brain matters. Surround yourself with stories of progress, not panic.

Abundance thinking won't happen overnight. But with daily reps, it begins to reshape the way you see money, not as something you chase, but something you **direct**.

The Role of Friction Tactics in Behavior Change

Now let's shift from mindset to mechanics.

Even with the best intentions, modern life is full of spending traps: one-click checkouts, buy-now-pay-later offers, endless sales, and personalized ads. These systems are *engineered* for impulsivity.

Enter: **friction tactics**, your new secret weapon.

Friction tactics are small, intentional barriers that slow down your spending reflex. They don't prevent you from buying what you need; they simply **buy time** for your logical brain to re-engage.

Why does this matter?

Because most spending regret happens when the **primitive, reward-seeking part of your brain (the limbic system)** hijacks your decision-making before your prefrontal cortex (responsible for long-term thinking) can catch up.

Friction tactics create just enough delay to interrupt that loop.

Think of it like this: If your impulses are the gas pedal, friction is the brake.

Examples of Friction Tactics You Can Use Today

You don't need a complicated system, just a few well-placed speed bumps between you and your spending urges. Here are proven tactics:

- **Unsubscribe from Marketing Emails**
  Out of sight, out of cart. Reducing exposure to sales triggers reduces temptations you didn't even want.

- **Delete Saved Payment Methods**
  If buying something online requires manually entering your card, it gives you a moment to reconsider. That moment is gold.

- **Use the 24-Hour Rule**
  For non-essential purchases, create a rule: wait 24 hours before buying. Most of the time, the urge will pass, and you'll thank yourself.

- **Use Cash for Discretionary Spending**
  Physically handing over cash makes spending more *real.* You're more likely to consider if it's worth it.

- **Automate Savings Before You Spend**
  Set up auto-transfers to savings right after payday. It creates friction by removing that money from easy access and builds

the habit of paying yourself first.

Friction isn't about restriction. It's about reflection.

Combining Abundance Thinking with Friction Tactics

Here's where the real transformation happens: when you **pair abundance thinking with friction tactics**.

Abundance gives you the *why*-the vision, the purpose, the future you're building.
Friction gives you the *how*-the guardrails, the tools, the pause that keeps you aligned.

Imagine this: You're tempted by a flash sale online. In the past, you'd click "Buy Now" without a second thought. But now? You've unsubscribed from email promos. You have to enter your card manually. Likewise, you remember your 24-hour rule. And you pause. In that pause, you reflect on your goal of saving for a trip next year. That trip feels more exciting than this impulse buy. You close the tab.

That's rewiring in real time. One decision at a time. One neural pathway at a time.

Abundance Thinking + Friction Tactics: The Mindset and Mechanics of Wealth

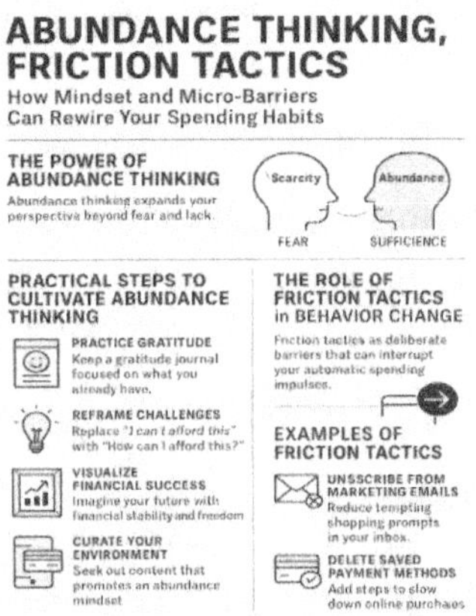

This visual guide distills the core ideas from Subchapter 6.1- how combining a mindset of abundance with simple friction tactics can interrupt impulsive spending, promote intentional decisions, and rewire your brain for financial success. Keep it nearby as a reminder that lasting wealth starts with how you think and what you pause before you buy.

Closing Thoughts: Transforming Mindsets and Habits

Abundance thinking and friction tactics aren't about saying "no" to everything. They're about saying "yes" to the things that truly matter.

They empower you to step out of autopilot and into ownership.

When you shift your mindset from scarcity to abundance, and back it up with small, strategic barriers, you take control of your behavior, and your future. You stop reacting. You start designing.

This isn't just about saving more or spending less. It's about **becoming the kind of person who makes decisions aligned with their values and long-term goals**.

Start small. Pick one abundance practice. Try one friction tactic. Let the rewiring begin.

Because wealth isn't just built in your bank account.

6.2: Tools: 30-Day Reset, Spending Strategy Map

Clear Habits, Clear Mind: How to Reboot and Rebuild Financial Behavior ?

You can't build long-term wealth on top of short-term chaos.

If you've ever tried to budget while still impulse spending, or set savings goals while feeling emotionally burnt out, you've felt the friction of trying to create financial order without clearing the clutter first. That's where this subchapter comes in.

Now that you've learned how abundance thinking and friction tactics can help rewire your spending habits, it's time to give your new mindset a structure, something concrete to follow when motivation dips or decision fatigue creeps in.

In this section, you'll learn two practical tools designed to do exactly that:

- The **30-Day Reset**: A behavioral reboot to clear out unhelpful spending patterns and recalibrate your financial awareness.

- The **Spending Strategy Map**: A flexible, visual plan to align your money with your values and priorities? So you're not just tracking spending, but guiding it.

Together, these tools act as the "implementation system" behind your rewired brain.

The 30-Day Reset: A Behavioral Cleanse for Your Wallet

Think of this like a detox? not from food, but from unconscious financial autopilot. The 30-Day Reset is designed to interrupt spending loops, increase mindfulness, and rebuild your relationship with money from the ground up.

What Is It?

The 30-Day Reset is a personal challenge where you commit to one month of intentional, restricted spending with three simple rules:

1. **Essential Only**: Spend only on true essentials? Rent, groceries, bills, medications.

2. **No New Discretionary Purchases**: Pause all non-essential buys (e.g., clothes, gadgets, takeout, entertainment).

3. **Track Every Expense**: Keep a simple daily log of what you spend and how it made you feel.

Why It Works (Behavioral Science Behind It):

- **Breaks automaticity**: Habit research shows that abstaining from a behavior for several weeks helps weaken the neural cue-behavior loop.

- **Restores conscious control**: Tracking your emotional response builds financial self-awareness, critical for long-term habit change.

- **Rebuilds dopamine tolerance**: If your brain has gotten used to frequent small rewards (e.g., shopping, takeout), taking a break helps recalibrate your reward system and reduce impulsive cravings.

Optional Enhancements:

- **Cash envelope for essentials**: Use cash for groceries or gas to make spending feel more tangible.

- **Journaling prompt**: End each day with one reflection: *"What did I learn about my spending triggers today?"*

- **Accountability buddy**: Partner with a friend or partner doing the challenge to share progress and stay motivated.

The Goal:

The goal isn't austerity, it's clarity. After 30 days, you'll have a clean behavioral slate and better insight into what you truly value.

The Spending Strategy Map: A Visual Plan for Purposeful Money Use

Once the Reset clears the fog, the Spending Strategy Map gives you the road.

Why Most Budgets Fail

Most people start budgeting from a place of restriction, cut this, limit that. But budgeting without strategy is like trying to diet without understanding nutrition. You might reduce calories, but you're still starving your goals.

The Spending Strategy Map flips that. Instead of telling your money where not to go, it tells your money where it *wants* to go, based on your real priorities.

Step 1: Identify Your Core Spending Values

Ask yourself:

- What do I truly value spending money on?
- What spending leaves me energized versus what leaves me regretful?

Use these categories to build your "value buckets," such as:

- Growth (education, courses, investing)
- Health (food, fitness, therapy)
- Freedom (savings, debt payoff)
- Connection (experiences, giving)

- Maintenance (essentials like rent, transportation)

Step 2: Map Fixed vs. Flexible

Draw two columns:

- **Fixed**: Non-negotiables like rent, insurance, debt payments.
- **Flexible**: Everything else, where intentionality can shine.

Assign percentages to each "value bucket" in your flexible column, based on what matters most. Example:

- Growth – 20%
- Health – 15%
- Freedom – 25%
- Connection – 10%
- Discretionary – 30%

Step 3: Automate + Monitor

Use automation (auto-transfers, direct debits) to push money into buckets like savings or investments first, *pay your priorities before your impulses.*

Then, do a quick weekly check-in:

- Am I staying true to my values?

- What category felt the most aligned this week? The least?

This turns your spending plan into a feedback loop, not a guilt trap.

Why These Tools Work Together ?

- **The 30-Day Reset** clears space in your neural and emotional system, it's a pattern interrupt.

- **The Spending Strategy Map** fills that space with alignment, structure, and purpose, it's a pattern installer.

One removes the weeds. The other plants, in the garden.

Using both, you're not just managing money, you're reshaping your identity: from spender to strategist, from reactive to intentional.

Reset & Realign: The 30-Day Reset + Spending Strategy Map

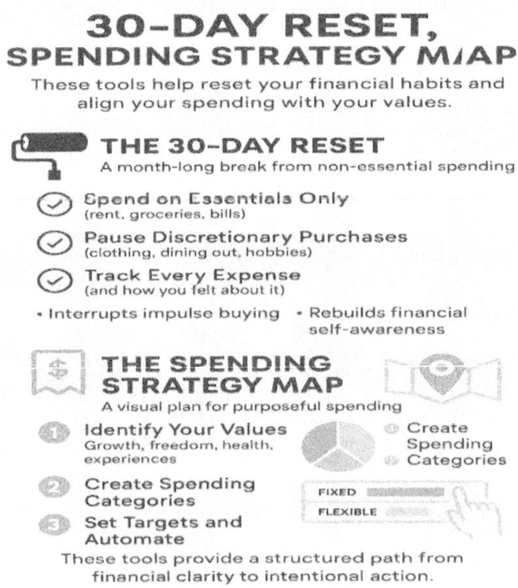

This visual guide captures the essence of two transformative tools: the 30-Day Reset to interrupt autopilot spending and restore financial clarity, and the Spending Strategy Map to align money with what truly matters. Use it as a quick reference to stay intentional, grounded, and goal-driven in your financial journey.

Final Thoughts: Build Habits That Build Wealth

Wealth isn't a product of willpower. It's a product of systems, and systems are built on habits.

The 30-Day Reset and Spending Strategy Map are two tools you can return to again and again. Anytime your finances feel off course, these tools help you re-center. When life gets busy, they bring focus. When you're tempted by impulse or scarcity, they bring intention.

You don't need perfection. You need practice.

One clear month. One clear map. That's where the shift begins.

CONCLUSION: Your Money, Your Mind, Your Power

How to maintain progress and embody a new financial identity? What if your next dollar wasn't just something to spend or save, but a statement of who you're becoming?

By now, you've looked beneath the surface of your spending. You've explored the invisible triggers, emotional, psychological, environmental, that shape your financial behavior more than spreadsheets or salary ever could. You've seen how stress, guilt, celebration, even boredom can tug at your wallet before your rational mind has a chance to speak. You've met your biases: optimism, FOMO, sunk cost fallacies that nudge you toward choices you wouldn't make with a clear head. You've seen how stores and screens are engineered to hijack your attention, and how your brain sometimes confuses dopamine with meaning.

And maybe, just maybe, you've started to realize something powerful:

Money is not just about math. It's about identity.

The Old Story: Spending Without Seeing

For most people, money is a story they didn't write. It's inherited beliefs ("Money doesn't grow on trees"), subtle cues from childhood ("We can't afford that"), and emotional coping mechanisms ("I deserve this after today"). It's years of habits formed in the shadows of stress, shame, or survival.

You've seen how spending patterns are often less about choice and more about *conditioning*. Marketers understand this. Algorithms exploit this. But now, you do, too.

And that awareness is your leverage. Because you can't change what you can't see.

The New Story: Rewiring from the Inside Out

This book hasn't been about perfection. It's been about permission.

Permission to pause.
Permission to feel what's underneath the urge to spend.
Permission to tell yourself a new story, one not rooted in fear, but in agency.

When you recognize that your brain is *plastic*, capable of rewiring, you stop beating yourself up for past mistakes and start building new circuits. You stop seeing a budget as a punishment and start seeing it as a mirror. You realize that every choice is a vote for the kind of person you're becoming.

Financial transformation isn't about willpower. It's about identity shift.
It's when you move from "I'm bad with money" to "I'm becoming someone who honors their money."
From "I'll never get ahead" to "I'm learning to align my money with what matters."

That's not wishful thinking. That's neuroplasticity, applied with purpose.

You Don't Need to Hustle, You Need to Align

Many books will tell you to work harder, cut more, optimize relentlessly. But what if the answer isn't hustle, it's *alignment*?

When your money habits reflect your values, discipline becomes less exhausting. You don't have to "force" yourself to save when you believe you're building something that matters. You don't have to resist every impulse when you know your future self deserves respect, not deprivation.

Alignment is when your inner world matches your outer choices.
That's the real definition of wealth.

Your Identity Is the Root of Your Habits

The most lasting change happens when you stop asking, *"What should I do?"* and start asking, *"Who am I becoming?"*

- The person who unsubscribes from marketing emails is saying, "I protect my peace."

- The person who automates savings is saying, "I take care of my future."

- The person who pauses before a purchase is saying, "I am intentional with my energy."

These small actions are not just tools, they're identity builders. And every time you act in alignment with the person you want to be, you reinforce that identity. One decision at a time.

Keep Going. Gently, But Relentlessly.

Progress won't always be linear. You will backslide. You will forget. You will overspend, overreact, overthink. That's not failure. That's being human.

But now you know how to return to yourself. You know how to pause. To reflect. To reconnect.

Don't let a setback become a sentence. Let it be a signal. Return to your HALT + B framework. Revisit your Spending Strategy Map. Reflect on what you're feeling, not just what you're buying. Let your brain catch up with your heart.

And then begin again.

A Final Invitation

You don't need to be rich to feel financially powerful. You need clarity. You need connection. You need intention.

Your money is not just a tool. It's a mirror. It reflects your fears, yes, but also your values, your growth, your courage.

So take up space in your financial life. Speak up. Slow down. Spend on purpose. Save with pride. Build a life that reflects who you *really* are, not who advertisers want you to be.

You are not behind. You are not broken.
You are becoming. You are aware. You are in motion.

This is your money. This is your mind. This is your power.

Go live like it.

www.ingramcontent.com/pod-product-compliance
Lightning Source LLC
LaVergne TN
LVHW022108200926
848481LV00003B/1097
9798231089369